No Strings Attached:
Untangling the Risks of Fundraising & Collaboration

by Melanie L. Herman and
Dennis M. Kirschbaum, ARM

Copyright © 1999
by the Nonprofit Risk Management Center

All Rights Reserved.

ISBN 1-893210-04-9

Nonprofit Risk Management Center
1001 Connecticut Avenue, NW
Suite 410
Washington, DC 20036
(202) 785-3891
Fax: (202) 296-0349
http://www.nonprofitrisk.org

About the Nonprofit Risk Management Center

The Nonprofit Risk Management Center is dedicated to helping community-serving nonprofits prevent harm, conserve resources, preserve assets, and free up resources for mission-critical activities. The Center provides technical assistance on risk management, liability, and insurance matters; publishes easy-to-use written materials; designs and delivers workshops and conferences; and offers competitively priced consulting services.

The Center is an independent nonprofit organization that does not sell insurance or endorse specific insurance providers. For more information on the products and services available from the Center, call (202) 785-3891 or visit our web site at http://www.nonprofitrisk.org.

Copyright © 1999 by the Nonprofit Risk Management Center

All rights reserved. ISBN 1-893210-04-9

Acknowledgments

The authors are grateful to the following persons who provided thoughtful comments and suggestions on the draft of this publication:

H. Felix Kloman, *Risk Management Reports*

Matthew Landy, *National Charities Information Bureau*

Sarah C. Varner, *Giorsi & Sorrenti, Inc.*

This publication is designed to provide accurate and authoritative information in regard to the subject matter covered. It is distributed with the understanding that the publisher is not engaged in rendering legal, accounting, or other professional service. If legal advice or other expert assistance is required, the services of a competent professional should be sought. From a Declaration of Principles jointly adopted by a Committee of the American Bar Association and a Committee of Publishers.

Table of Contents

Introduction 1

Chapter 1   Fundraising and Risk Management:
Unraveling the Mysteries 7

Chapter 2   The Budget: The Tie That Binds 19

Chapter 3   Foundation Grants: Casting a Wide Net 31

Chapter 4   Individual Donors: Roping 'Em In 37

Chapter 5   Corporate Support: Safety Net or Spider's Web? 55

Chapter 6   Collaborations and Partnerships: Creating a Secure Knot 63

Chapter 7   Toeing the Line: Managing Within the Restrictions
of Your Grant or Contract and the Law 71

Chapter 8   Resources 81

Appendix A   National Society of Fund Raising Executives'
Code of Ethical Principles and Standards of Professional Practice ... 85

Appendix B   National Charities Information Bureau
Standards in Philanthropy 89

Charities rely on donations voluntarily given. In a transaction between a charity and a donor, the value that passes from one to the other is the promise that the service for which the donor implicitly contracted will, in fact be delivered by the charity. The service recipient is society, a community or a party unknown (and frequently unidentified) to the donor. The donor's belief that the charity will use the contribution purposefully, effectively and efficiently for the charitable mission is the foundation of the philanthropic exchange.

(Source: *National Society for Fund Raising Executives*)

Introduction

It is often said that there is no such thing as a free lunch. When someone gives something to your organization, they almost always expect something in return. Sometimes all they wish is for their donation to be acknowledged and appreciated. Others may require much more. This is not intrinsically wrong or unethical but difficulties can arise when both sides are not clear on exactly what the expectations are. If expectations on both sides are communicated fully and agreed upon in advance, it is much less likely that problems or misunderstandings will occur later on.

Fundraising in a nonprofit organization is like a beating heart in the human body — it enables the circulation of financial resources to provide service delivery to the far reaches of the organization. When the beating stops, even if momentarily during a transition of leadership, the organization may suffer serious, if not irreparable, damage. When the top position at a small nonprofit is vacated, the board must act swiftly to replace the outgoing CEO, or risk losing precious time on the fundraising calendar. Most CEOs describe their fundraising activities as an ongoing activity. Environmental conditions such as the organization's good reputation in the community, the availability of capable volunteers to lead a fundraising campaign, and changed priorities of a major donor, can also affect the nonprofit's ability to raise the funds necessary for survival and ultimate success.

Most nonprofit CEOs view fundraising as an integral and necessary activity. It has to be done. Some cynically or pessimistically view it as a necessary evil. Others approach fundraising with the enthusiasm of a youth sports coach, seeing a dual role of getting the job done and rallying the team needed to support the effort. And fundraising exhilarates a smaller number of CEOs who see the process as an elaborate puzzle or challenging game. Some nonprofit executives experience all of these viewpoints as they pursue the elusive dollars needed to keep their charities afloat. Whether you approach fundraising with cynicism or excitement, it is essential that you understand the importance of fundraising and consider its risks in addition to the rewards in your efforts to keep the heart of your organization steadily beating.

Your Organization's Reputation: A Pearl Beyond Price

In most cases, the asset at greatest risk in a fundraising activity is an intangible one: your nonprofit's reputation. Preservation of reputation, stature, and credibility is one of the weightiest burdens on a nonprofit CEO. Without this priceless asset, most nonprofits would find it impossible to survive. The downfall of many nonprofits can be attributed to the erosion of reputation. During the past decade, the fundraising follies, ethical missteps, and collaboration catastrophes of countless nonprofits have made headlines. These scandals have had positive and negative effects on the nonprofit sector. On the positive side, the call for accountable organizations emerging from the dust of scandal is causing a growing number of nonprofits to look inward at their practices and identify long-standing weaknesses that require adjustment. The call for accountability has led to better run, more responsible organizations that give stakeholder concerns and expectations the serious attention they deserve.

Unfortunately, these scandals have cast a pall on the nonprofit world negating the tremendous work and contributions made by so many charitable organizations. This latter phenomenon has made it more difficult for nonprofits to sustain their support. Funders and supporters have become increasingly cynical and a nonprofit must now convince a potential supporter that not only is its service delivery worthwhile, but also that the organization is administered responsibly and is deserving of charitable support. On top of that, the nonprofit sector continues to grow at an unprecedented rate. Recent estimates place the number of charitable nonprofits at more than 600,000, with the total number of nonprofits nationwide exceeding 1.5 million. No slowdown in growth is expected in the years ahead as governments continue to devolve service delivery and boundaries of what constitutes a nonprofit continue to expand. That means that competition for a limited pool of funds will grow more vigorous every year.

The purpose of this book is first to raise the consciousness of nonprofit fundraisers throughout the sector about the risks that accompany the rewards of fundraising. Second, we hope to provide a practical framework through which nonprofit CEOs, boards, and others engaged in fundraising can address the risks and move forward responsibly. It is not our intent to discourage any of the forms of fundraising discussed in the text. Rather, we hope to inspire those engaged in fundraising to approach this vital, important work with greater responsibility and care. To be engaged in the business of nonprofit fundraising is to grapple continuously with challenges. Ethics, common sense, and a realistic attitude are necessary to survive. It is our hope that this book will increase awareness about these sometimes difficult issues while helping the reader to find that although there still is no such thing as a free lunch, you can at least get what you pay for.

In Chapter 1 we consider the risks associated with raising funds. Current giving trends and the growth of the nonprofit sector are just two of the factors affecting fundraising. We also explore the role of the board and others in your nonprofit's fundraising efforts.

In Chapter 2 we explore the foundation of every fundraising program, the budget. How should you approach the budgeting process to reduce the likelihood of falling short of your goals? How should a nonprofit balance the need to be ambitious and realistic in projecting fundraising outcomes?

In Chapter 3 we take a closer look at the solicitation of foundation grants. Has raising funds from foundations changed significantly in recent years? Are there special risks associated with raising money from foundations, large and small, national and community-based?

In Chapter 4 we look at individual donors. Individuals contribute an estimated 85 percent of all of charitable donations. Individual donors range from active volunteers to anonymous benefactors. Donations come in the form of cash, checks, and pledges for ongoing support to gifts of equipment, property, stocks, or estate proceeds. Soliciting money from individuals has become hugely complex in an era of sophisticated, personalized direct mail, and with the availability of charitable remainder trusts and other instruments that facilitate a range of deferred or planned giving.

In Chapter 5 we look at corporate support. Critics of the proliferation of corporate support programs decry the commercialization of the charitable sector through corporate sponsorship of youth recreation programs, public schools, mentoring programs, and other activities that have historically been free from commercial sponsorship. But the lure of corporate support is compelling for nonprofits that are facing stiff competition, the loss of government funds, or lack of resources needed to start a sophisticated direct mail campaign.

In Chapter 6 we explore the rapidly changing world of collaborations and partnerships. The exponential growth of the nonprofit sector has been matched by the phenomenon of joint ventures, partnerships, and other relationships. Nonprofits are working with other nonprofits, public entities, and corporations. These collaborations often enable nonprofits to reach new clients, expand service delivery, or increase efficiency. Many develop at the urging of traditional foundation funders, who see the potential benefits of partnerships. Collaborations and partnerships represent an exciting frontier for many nonprofits, but they are also risky. We'll explore several ways to minimize the risk of surprise, disappointment, or crisis and improve the chances that all parties to a collaborative venture will be satisfied with the outcome.

In Chapter 7 we examine the challenges presented by restricted funding, including government and private grants. Many fundraisers bemoan the declining number of funders providing unrestricted grants for a nonprofit's overall operations. Funders cite their interest in supporting innovative approaches to problem solving as the top reason for restricting grants to a specific purpose. Each nonprofit should have a strategy in place for managing restricted funding, before it solicits these funds. Two unsuccessful dynamics are common: first, nonprofits may try to couch general operations as innovative projects in order to gain access to restricted grant funds, and second, nonprofits may scramble to come up with innovative programs and projects that somehow address the organization's core mission. This posturing may heighten risk as the emphasis on gamesmanship overshadows an honest accounting of the strings that accompany restricted funding. In this chapter we will suggest a strategy for evaluating your readiness to manage restricted funds and meet the intricate web of donor./funder-imposed requirements.

Chapter 8 contains a list of resources, including organizations, publications, and web sites. We urge readers to refer to these resources — many are free — as you develop a strategy for managing fundraising risk in your nonprofit.

Finally, two useful reference documents are featured as appendices:

- ❑ the National Society of Fund Raising Executives' *Code of Ethical Principles and Standards of Professional Practice;* and
- ❑ the National Charities Information Bureau *Standards in Philanthropy.*

Chapter 1
Fundraising and Risk Management: Unraveling the Mysteries

Fundraising in the Nonprofit Sector – Trends to Consider

As we look at the business of fundraising at the beginning of the new century, several trends are quite apparent:

- Competition for funding is increasingly fierce among a growing number of nonprofits. Estimates are that there are now more than 1.5 million nonprofits in the U.S. alone. The charitable sector is the fastest growing sector in our economy.

- The pressure to diversify an organization's funding sources and avoid reliance on one or two sources of funds is greater than ever. Nonprofits that rely exclusively on one or two sources of funds are at great risk.

- Sector experts report a slowing of growth in total giving based on a recent decline in corporate giving, and a projected continuing decline in government support for social services delivery.

- Meeting the wide-ranging requirements and expectations of a diverse pool of funders is necessary but difficult. Simply tracking the reporting requirements and filing deadlines of funders can be quite time consuming. This burden is likely to continue as funders in all categories demand additional accountability from the charities they support.

- Most nonprofits operate in small communities, where there are limited sources of funding for charitable activities.

- Healthy nonprofits must pursue diversification of revenues as well as steady growth in overall fundraising results, in order to maintain services. Nonprofit expenses grow, on average, 5-10 percent per year. Fundraising proceeds must keep pace or an organization is at risk of financial catastrophe.

- Funders are consolidating their giving as never before — many report the desire to focus grantmaking on one or more specific areas. They are also sending signals that they want nonprofits to collaborate in presenting proposals, and in some cases, consider mergers and consolidations.

- Successful nonprofits are engaged in "niche" marketing: reaching out to specific types of businesses, making an effort to understand the interests of each company, and forging partnerships that benefit the company, the nonprofit, and the community.

- Marketing and fundraising appeals are becoming more sophisticated and more targeted.

- Special events fundraising has grown quickly, creating frustration on the part of donors and saturating the market.

- Given competing demands on donors from an enormous and growing community of charities, nonprofits can no longer assume the renewal of last year's personal donations, corporate donations, or foundation grants.

- Cause-related marketing alliances are an increasingly popular fundraising strategy, providing nonprofits with access to substantial corporate marketing budgets.

What Could Go Wrong?

Most nonprofits embarking on a risk management program look first to the critical areas of client safety and risk financing (insurance). The issues of volunteer screening, employment practices, and transportation safety may subsequently appear on the radar screen. Few managers think of fundraising as an operational area fraught with risk. Upon closer scrutiny, however, a range of risks emerge. Here are some examples.

- ❑ Proceeds from this year's fundraising campaign fall short of a nonprofit's unrealistic projections.

- ❑ An unhappy donor sues to get his substantial donation back when a school fails to use the donation to build a new facility within a specified time frame.

- ❑ A large association abruptly cancels a cause-related marketing venture with a manufacturer following public outcry about the ethical dilemmas inherent in the relationship and is sued by the manufacturer for breach of contract.

- ❑ A charity falters after the publication of an article alleging that young service recipients depicted in the organization's fundraising materials have long since died.

- ❑ A nonprofit that relies on government funds prepares to close its doors when the government fails to make timely payments on its contract.

- ❑ A local mentoring program receives a restricted grant from a community foundation to fund the expansion of its mentoring program to serve kids who have a history of violence. The funder elects not to renew its commitment, but the executive director vows to continue the program despite the lack of funding.

- ❏ The executive director of a community-based nonprofit accepts a major grant from an aluminum container producer. The grant is intended for use in underwriting a school-based educational program. The board splits on whether or not to accept the gift, with some arguing about the need for revenues and new partners, and others concerned about being a front for corporate interests. Both factions frame their arguments in terms of the organization's mission.

- ❏ A homeless shelter is unable to afford the cost of a full-time fundraiser and instead hires a development officer who is paid a percentage of the money she raises for the agency. A major contributor later learns that 25 cents of every dollar raised during the campaign was remitted to the professional fundraiser in the form of a commission. He expresses dismay at the high cost of the campaign and use of his donation.

- ❏ A public radio station shares its list of donors with a political party and opens itself to congressional and press scrutiny.

If some of these scenarios sound familiar, it's because they're drawn from recent headlines and media reports. Could your nonprofit organization find itself in any of these situations? The messages should be clear that regardless of your organization's size or the population that you serve, the risks of fundraising are present even if you are in complete compliance with the letter of the law.

What is Risk Management?

Risk is the possible deviation from what you expect to occur. It can be either better or worse than what you anticipate. In most cases, you should focus greatest attention on the threats to the ability of your nonprofit to achieve its mission. For example, something, known or unknown, that could impair your ability to recruit volunteers, serve clients, advocate a point of view, facilitate networking, or educate your constituency. Risk management is a discipline for dealing with uncertainty. Effective risk management increases the probability of successfully attaining goals and fulfilling your mission by allowing you to anticipate future constraints and barriers, and plan alternatives around those barriers. To manage the risks in your nonprofit you need to ask and answer three questions about every aspect of your operation:

1. What could go wrong?

2. What will we do? (both to prevent harm and in the aftermath of an incident)

3. How will we pay for it?

The "bottom-line" of risk management in the nonprofit sector is to maintain the public confidence. Truly effective nonprofits consider the risk management questions above in the context of every major aspect of their organization and for most nonprofits a major functional area is fundraising. Too often, an effort to control risk in our organizations is an effort to control costs. Managing spending, maintaining financial controls, and keeping a keen eye on the expenses is often what passes for fiscal responsibility. Important as that is, if the other side of the equation, the revenue side, is ignored we are missing half of the picture.

Let's face it, though we are not in business to turn a profit, most years the bottom line must be printed in black ink if our organizations are to continue for very long. Some of the specific areas every nonprofit should consider in evaluating and managing fundraising activities are addressed in the chapters that follow.

Getting the Right People Involved

Ultimately it is the board of directors and the chief executive who are responsible for raising money for your nonprofit. Though you may decide to delegate responsibility for raising grant monies to a professional fundraiser, it is clear that he or she will never have the vested interest in the outcome that you will have. You can pay someone to do a job, but you can't pay someone to take ownership of the organization. Here's what two industry groups are saying:

> "Board members are the primary stewards of the nonprofit organization, ultimately responsible for securing adequate resources and overseeing the disposition of those resources." *Source: National Center for Nonprofit Boards*

> "To be ethical, philanthropic fundraising must be mission-led, institutionally-based, volunteer-driven and professionally supported in an environment free of improper motive, unreasonable reward, or personal inurement." *Source: National Society of Fund Raising Executives*

Practically speaking, what can individual board members do to create an environment in which funders understand the organization's mission and feel comfortable supporting it? We present a few ideas on this topic over the next several pages.

The Board's Role in Fundraising

Nonprofit board members:

- ✓ determine what is really possible to achieve by participating in planning activities;
- ✓ open doors and make introductions;
- ✓ cultivate and influence potential donors;
- ✓ monitor and guide fundraising initiatives;
- ✓ demonstrate commitment to the organization by example of their own giving; and

- consider and review the organization's "case statement" (why the organization needs money and how it will be used).

In some organizations there may also be a need for a Fund Development Committee, a group of dedicated individuals drawn from staff, the board and the general public that focuses on guiding the fundraising activities of the charity. Here are some of their areas of concern.

The Fund Development Committee

The committee:

- serves as the board's agent to coordinate the work of the board members, CEO and fundraising staff;
- reminds all boards members of their responsibilities;
- helps the organization focus on its strengths and mission;
- helps ensure good stewardship of donations and grants;
- assists in the development of strategies for involving the entire board in fundraising;
- serves as a source of information on factors affecting fund-raising among the organization's constituents; and
- solicits gifts at various levels required for ongoing and special fundraising efforts.

Staffing the Fundraising Program

Who will do the actual work of fundraising? Usually there is a team of people — each of whom brings different skills and specialized knowledge to the task. Here are some of the people typically involved.

1. **Existing staff**. When there is a strong need to build institutional capacity to raise funds, one answer is to train current staff or hire new staff with the skills and expertise the organization needs.

2. **Professional fundraisers**. A professional fundraiser can be a tremendous boon to a small or medium-sized organization, which may lack the knowledge and expertise of this often complex and seemingly mysterious field. It is important to remember that a conscientious professional is guided by the highest ethical standards. Even so, the board and staff still have an obligation to monitor and review the professional's activities closely. Also, it is foolish and irresponsible to expect that a professional fundraiser can solve an organization's financial woes, or bring in huge sums of money without a high level of support and involvement from key stakeholders in the organization, including the staff and board.

3. **Temporary staff**. Where the need is short-term but a sustained effort must be made for a limited period of time, a temporary fundraising staff may be an appropriate alternative.

4. **Volunteers**. Many nonprofits use volunteers including board members, committee members, and others to supplement staff to take on this work. It is important to remember, however, that volunteers often have professional and personal commitments of their own that may limit their ability to give this vital area their undivided attention. The result may be that goals, essential to the organization's survival, are not met. In other cases, volunteers who also contribute funds to the organization may be a nonprofit's most persuasive and effective fundraisers.

The question of whether or not to hire a professional fundraiser deserves some extra attention as it is a complex issue with no single right answer for every organization.

It can often be helpful and necessary to recruit some expertise either on a staff or contract basis. The professional fundraiser provides the benefit of specialized skill and expertise in fundraising. As nonprofit organizations in recent years have tried to model themselves on for-profit organizations, some have considered paying fundraisers on commission or a percentage of income generated.

The National Society of Fund Raising Executives (NSFRE), an association of fundraising professionals, has looked closely at this issue. NSFRE has developed guidelines which specify that such compensation is not appropriate in a nonprofit environment for a variety of reasons.

The guiding principle behind these guidelines is that those involved with nonprofits must not enjoy personal inurement as a result of their connection with the nonprofit. (Compensation based on skill, effort and time expended, remunerated by salary or fee, does not constitute personal inurement.) According to NSFRE, commission or percentage compensation breaches the "no-inurement" principle and is therefore inherently unethical because:

1. The mission and long-term interests of the charity may become secondary to the worker's personal interest and self-gain. The donor's (and public's) interests and needs may no longer be foremost.

2. Donor attitudes can be unalterably damaged in reaction to the awareness that a direct commission will be paid to a fundraiser from his or her gift, thus compromising the trust on which charity relies.

3. Percentage or commission compensation can foster unethical behavior or inappropriate conduct by individuals whose self-interest is oriented to immediate results, irrespective of the donor's best interest.

4. Fundraising is an ongoing process of donor identification and cultivation. Individuals develop an affinity for an organizational mission and wish to further it through charitable contributions. A major tenet for success is that

an organization is strengthened when volunteers are actively involved in this process.

The role of a professional fundraiser should include building an increasingly committed, enthusiastic and capable group of volunteers. Tying compensation to commission may discourage this activity.

5. Commission and percentage compensation can provide reward without merit. Contributions that materialize at a given moment are often the culmination of the efforts of many people, including volunteers, over a long period of time. The person whose compensation rests on commission or percentage would wish to include such gifts within calculations for his or her compensation.

6. Donors' interests may not remain paramount. There are a variety of donative paths and financial instruments from which contributors may choose. The percentage-paid fundraiser may influence donor choice so as to generate the greatest current result, rather than preserve the donor's assets for the best long-term benefit to him or her, and to the charity.[1]

Although the principle of no commission has remained firmly in place, in recent years the NSFRE has softened its position somewhat on merit pay and bonuses for fundraising executives. Clearly, this is a complex area and much thought should be given to how a fundraiser will be compensated before he or she is brought on board.

In the remaining chapters of this book, we will explore some of the potential negative consequences of fundraising efforts. We will also outline specific steps to mitigate risk and ensure that your well-intentioned efforts yield the results you expect and require.

---

[1] *Source: the National Society of Fund Raising Executives*

Mitigation is particularly crucial to fundraising, as your risk financing options are limited. Risk financing involves answering the question: "How will we pay for it?" before harm or loss occurs. There are no insurance policies available that will compensate a nonprofit for falling short of ambitious fundraising projections, or restore a reputation damaged by a questionable partnership. The only real option is to dig in, and to rebuild your nonprofit's reputation.

Chapter 2
The Budget:
The Tie That Binds

In his book *The New-York Historical Society*, Kevin Guthrie chronicles the history of a revered New York charity founded in 1804 to "collect and preserve materials relating to the early history of New York and the United States." In telling the story of the Society's roller-coaster ride through financial hardship, intense media coverage, and a shifting mission, Guthrie draws attention to a multitude of management and leadership practices that contributed to a major disruption for the institution. In addition to the unique, outsider's perspective he brings to the story, Guthrie describes many practices each of which might cripple a typical nonprofit. One of the areas illuminated in the book is the Society's annual budgeting process.

Guthrie outlines various financial management practices that were risky and dangerous for the Society. Many readers will find little similarity between some of these practices and those of their own organizations. The issue of budget development, however, is common to all nonprofits. Every organization must base both its fundraising and spending on projections of revenue and expenditures in order to be healthy. The Society was guilty of a budgeting mistake that is all too common on the nonprofit sector: beginning the process on the wrong side of the page. In other words, starting the annual budget process by calculating the expense side of the budget.

It is certainly easier to begin with expenses. One lists this year's expenses, and calculates increases based on known factors such as a timed rent escalation, higher postage costs, across the board salary increases of 5 percent, the addition of programs and services, higher printing costs due to anticipated growth in a mailing list, etc. Even without adding new services or expanding a client base, the typical nonprofit's expenses grow by five percent per year due to inflation, salary adjustments, and other increases.

So it's not difficult to come up with apparently realistic and logical projections on the expense side of the budget. At the end of the process, the CEO has produced a list of "what we need." And, he or she has also produced, through the magic of a spreadsheet or perhaps a simple calculator — the magic number — the sum of money that must be raised to meet the coming year's expenses. So now he or she turns his or her attention to the revenue side of the budget. The remaining step in the budgeting process is simply getting the columns of support — individual donations, foundation grants, corporate support, fees, sales revenue, etc. — to add up to the "magic number," plus in some cases, additional for a cushion or projected net income for the year. The danger in this approach should be clear: it easily leads to unrealistic revenue projections. Arguably, it predestines the revenue number, which must be at least the magic number.

Realism is required on both sides of the budget. The failure to adequately forecast revenues or expenses may spell unrecoverable disaster for a nonprofit. For small organizations, immediate survival in the face of a deficit may be impossible. In larger institutions like the Historical Society, the availability of an endowment or other source of funding may cushion or delay the impact of unrealistic projections.

In the case of the New-York Historical Society, Guthrie illustrates the necessity to start the budgeting process on the revenue side, asking first: what can we realistically hope to raise next year? — before asking "how will we use these revenues to fulfill our mission?" This sounds like an overly simplistic solution to the understandably complex challenge of fortifying a nonprofit organization. Its simplicity does not make it any easier for the person developing next year's budget. It's so much easier to start with "what we need to run the organization" than face the agonizing decisions necessary when the same or less revenue is expected next year than was generated this year.

For example, an educational charity experienced a banner year selling instructional materials. Additional staff, equipment and materials were acquired to support this expanded operation. The proper approach to the budget requires starting with the question: "Is it realistic to expect similar performance next year, or was there some factor that made these results extraordinary, such as something happening in the community that was beyond our control?" If it is not realistic to project continued growth, or in fact appropriate to project a lesser figure, then the budgeted revenue must confront the infrastructure issues on the expense side of the budget.

Risk Management Checklist

- ❑ *Begin the budgeting process on the revenue side of the budget.* Always take into consideration the following:

    — Consider what is realistic and possible when establishing projections for each revenue category.

    — Think about special circumstances or environmental factors that resulted in anomalous results in the past year.

    — Consider special circumstances that may impede fundraising in the upcoming year (i.e. funder consolidation, change in focus or priorities, loss of key leaders).

    — Never use an arbitrary formula such as growth of five or ten percent in each revenue category to develop projections for next year.

    — Consider each category separately, and weigh the potential for fundraising honestly and carefully.

- *Carefully review your expense assumptions.*
    - Can staff be used more efficiently?
    - How could certain expenses be reduced or eliminated?
    - If there is a gap between income and expense, what is the right way to manage that gap? Very often a critical look at the budget will reveal the need to develop and diversify the organization's sources of income.

Achieving the Right Funding Mix: Diversifying the Revenue Side of the Page

How diverse should your sources of revenue be? Should you establish an endowment fund that will generate a stream of income for core services? There are no formulas or easy answers to these questions. Any manager who has seen a sudden decrease in donations, membership dues, venture income or major revenue-producing events such as a charity fundraiser or conference fall short of attendance expectations, can tell you the value of having several different sources of income. Most nonprofit organizations rely on several different revenue streams which may include: individual donations, membership dues, foundation grants, meeting/registration fees, product sales, corporate sponsorship revenues, contract fees, and fees for services.

The important thing to remember is that each of these sources of income arrives with its own set of responsibilities, obligations, and risks. For example, a membership organization must be accountable to its members, who may be viewed as the organization's owners. For a membership organization there is no specific number or percentage of dues to total income that is considered optimal.

On the other hand, a membership organization whose dues form too small a percentage of its overall revenue could risk losing sight of its mission, as it focuses more on meeting the expectations and desires of its principal sources of funding rather than on its mission. For example, an organization that is not overly scrupulous in accepting corporate donations might be diverted to helping those companies promote their products and services rather than focusing on its principal, community-serving mission.

In addition, each funding source may require different methods of administering and accounting for the funds. Government grants and contracts are particularly notorious for having strict guidelines for accounting and administration. Failure to comply with these requirements and restrictions could lead to financial and even criminal penalties. Be sure to look carefully at the administrative burden imposed by any source of funding before the funding is accepted. If the infrastructure to administer the grant or contract is not already in place, consider the costs in both dollars and staff time to create it.

On the whole, an organization is stronger if it has multiple sources of revenue and doesn't rely too heavily on any one source of income. Welcome to the complex and often risky world of fundraising where the financial needs of an organization must often be balanced against costs and compromises that go along with raising the needed cash.

Some of the questions an organization's staff and board need to consider before embarking on an aggressive fundraising campaign are:

- How much should we spend on fundraising efforts?
- Are donations enabling the organization to achieve its mission and deliver programs and services consistent with the mission or simply fueling a fundraising infrastructure?
- What are the risks of "under investing" in fundraising efforts? Is the organization spending enough?

- ❏ What is an acceptable or maximum percentage of total administrative costs that should be spent on fundraising? (How much are we willing to spend to make a dollar?)

- ❏ Do we have the professional resources in-house to appropriately monitor the requirements of current donors? Will this be true if our donor base expands?

- ❏ Have systems been established to ensure that we meet donor-imposed requirements and deadlines? Who is responsible for ensuring compliance?

Choosing Appropriate Fundraising Techniques

Every nonprofit should select the fundraising techniques that: enable the organization to achieve its mission, deliver core services, and meet fundraising goals; are cost-effective; are consistent with the organization's policies and culture; and are ethical and above reproach. Here are some examples of different approaches to fundraising.

■ Direct Marketing

Direct marketing is the solicitation, usually through the mail or by telephone, of products, services or donations through direct contact with the prospective buyer or donor. Advantages of direct mail include the opportunity to educate constituencies and to bring in new donors. Disadvantages include relatively high start-up costs, uncertain results and the risk of angering some donors who don't approve of such campaigns. Here are some issues to consider:

- ❏ Do we have access to a list of potential donors or clients?

- ❏ Can we afford this type of program?

- ❏ Has the organization registered in each and every state requiring registration, before the solicitation commences?

❑ Are there similar organizations in the community that have been successful with direct mail? If so, have we gathered information about these efforts?

❑ Do we have access to the mailing lists of similar organizations?

Another aspect of direct marketing is that it often takes multiple contacts with the same individuals before any appreciable results are seen. Consider whether you are prepared to make this kind of sustained effort.

■ Personal Solicitations

The most effective method of securing support is through a one-to-one request, ideally in person; alternately, by telephone. This personal communication enables the donor to ask questions freely and obtain more information about the organization and project than might be available from a written document. The risk to the organization is that the solicitor of the gift must be credible and knowledgeable about the organization and its programs. If the solicitor cannot answer the donor's questions, the donor may lose faith in the organization's ability to carry out the programs.

■ Earned and Venture Income

Earned income is revenue a nonprofit generates through program-related activities (such as membership or participation fees). Venture income is revenue from projects that are undertaken solely to generate new revenues (i.e. Girl Scout cookie sales). As a reminder, unrelated activities (those unrelated to the nonprofit's charitable mission) may not exceed 25 percent of total expenditures and effort, and no distribution of income may be made to members, directors, or officers.

■ Sponsorships of Conferences and Events

Offering private sector companies the opportunity to support your meetings and events by underwriting part of the cost has become a very popular way of supplementing the fees that attendees pay and keeping down the costs to the organization. Typically, anything from coffee breaks to luncheons to evening events can be sponsored. One enterprising organization even obtained a sponsor for paper clip holders which were given to annual conference attendees.

The sponsoring organization usually receives some public recognition or other perks for supporting a conference, meeting, or special event. This, however, is an area in which caution must be exercised. The Internal Revenue Service has determined in some sponsorship arrangements that the sponsor was in effect paying for advertising and required the nonprofit organization to pay taxes on the proceeds as income not related to its tax-exempt mission (see Chapter 7). The sponsorship of individual aspects of a meeting or conference, such as coffee breaks and giveaways, may create an overly commercial atmosphere to your proceedings. In some organizations attendees will react negatively when the host appears to have sold every available advertising opportunity. The risk is that your nonprofit may become better known for its commercial "endorsements" than for its primary mission. Your conference may remind attendees of watching an athletic event where the backdrop is covered with advertisements. Others will appreciate your efforts to keep the registration fee as low as possible. Gauging the reaction of participants is key to managing the risks of sponsorships.

■ Marketing ventures with for profit organizations

In exchange for use of a nonprofit's name, logo, or endorsement a business may contribute a portion of sales to the nonprofit organization. Cause-related marketing is one of the fastest growing areas of revenue generation for nonprofit organizations. Credit cards, insurance and financial services are among the most popular items but the names (and reputations) of nonprofits have been used to sell everything from appliances to over-the-counter medicines to granola bars. The potential risks of these arrangements to nonprofits are numerous, including the risk that a product bearing the organization's name, logo or endorsement may have problems, or that other potential donors will be unwilling to support the nonprofit because of its ties to a competitor. Risks and questions to be considered are discussed more fully in Chapter 5.

- **Paid advertising**

A nonprofit organization may sell advertising space in its publications or on its web site. Note: This is usually considered to be unrelated business income (UBI) and may be subject to tax. Information about unrelated business income must be reported to the IRS on a special tax return called the 990T.

- **Work for hire**

A nonprofit may agree to provide work or services to another organization under a contractual agreement. When considering contractual work, determine whether the work fits into the organization's mission, and meets critical client needs. Also evaluate whether the time required to complete the work could be better spent addressing key aspects of the organization's mission. Last, could the relationship between your nonprofit and the other organization be damaging in any way to your reputation or stature?

- **Special Events**

Special events can be a costly way to raise funds but may be appropriate especially when a secondary goal can be achieved. For example, the annual "Race for the Cure" held in cities across the country consistently grabs national media attention concerning the continuing risk of breast cancer.

- **Planned Giving**

Planned giving involves gifts of money, securities, or other property made by a donor for future or sometimes present use by the recipient nonprofit. Such gifts may include:

- ✓ *Life insurance*: The donor names the nonprofit as beneficiary and deducts the sum of paid premiums or cash value of the policy as charitable contributions for income tax purposes.

✓ *Gifts of property*: Donors makes irrevocable gifts and may receive fixed payments (income) for a lifetime or certain number of years. There may be upkeep and storage costs.

✓ *Gifts of real estate*: The donor makes outright gifts or "gifts of real estate with retained life estate," which enables a donor to donate a home but continue to live in it. The donor receives a tax deduction on the gift as well as any improvements he makes to the home while living in it.

✓ *Gift annuity*: Donors give cash, securities, real or personal property to a nonprofit and the charity makes fixed payments to the donor. A nonprofit can "reinsure" this annuity by selling it to a commercial carrier.

Risk Management Checklist

As you evaluate the feasibility of the various fundraising techniques described above, consider the following questions:

❑ Will this technique contribute to our efforts to carry out our mission — or simply generate funds for low-priority or unnecessary activities or services?

❑ What are the best and worst possible outcomes of this approach? Are we prepared for both?

❑ Will this approach enable the nonprofit to deliver additional services or reach a wider audience?

❑ How will others (donors, service recipients, the public, etc.) likely perceive our fundraising techniques, particularly in terms of our reputation?

❑ Is the proposed approach cost-effective? Do we have enough information about the strategy to evaluate whether it will be cost-effective? (Have we done our homework?)

- ❏ Does the technique require a long-term investment of time or substantial investment of resources? (For example, a capital campaign clearly requires a commitment over the long-haul. Experts also report that renting mailing lists to sell products or solicit donations requires multiple mailings to achieve a reasonable rate of return.)

- ❏ Is the technique consistent with our philosophy? (For example, an advocacy organization dedicated to raising awareness about consumer privacy might be ill-advised to sell its membership or donor list.)

- ❏ What time and resource commitments are we making to this approach? Do we currently have staff who are knowledgeable about this type of fundraising? If existing staff take on a new fundraising effort, what existing work will have to be reassigned or dropped? If we don't have the human resources we need, are we prepared to hire the expertise we need, on a permanent or temporary basis?

- ❏ What return on investment do we expect over what period of time? How will we evaluate success?

- ❏ Is the proposed fundraising approach ethical and above reproach?

Chapter 3
Foundation Grants: Casting a Wide Net

Private foundations can be a significant and important source of income for nonprofit organizations but finding the right foundations to help fund your organization is more of an art than a science. There are many factors that can determine whether a source of funding is right for your nonprofit and a host of other reasons that influence your chances of securing grant funding. It always makes sense to begin with foundations whose funding priorities and guidelines are compatible with the project you have in mind. Then, strive to creatively explain why you feel your nonprofit is a good match. It's rarely — if ever — appropriate to pursue funding when the funder's published guidelines are clearly outside the scope of your project. Once you identify some foundations you think would be strong potential contributors to your cause, you must convince a grant officer and often a review board of your case. Your relationship with the decision-maker will be the key factor in determining whether your organization is the recipient of a grant or a rejection letter. Increasing the chance of acceptance requires a multifaceted strategy that may include some of the following tactics:

- ❑ Ensure that the foundation's current funding priorities encompass the type of project you're trying to obtain funding for;
- ❑ Identify the key contact person for the type of project;

- ❑ Develop a relationship with the key contact or contacts at the grantmaking organization;

- ❑ Follow directions provided by the grantmaker (e.g. don't submit a full proposal when a letter of inquiry is called for);

- ❑ Identify credible, connected people who can vouch for the project or provide a timely endorsement of your organization's good works;

- ❑ Allow sufficient time for the review process — few grants with large foundations are awarded within a year from the date of first contact. Don't expect that you'll receive a check within 90 days of your letter of inquiry;

- ❑ Invest in relationships for the long-term. Remember that although an organization may not choose to fund a current proposal, the next submission may fit better with the foundation's goals.

Even when the grant check is finally in the mail, from a risk management perspective, your work is just beginning as you consider the possibility that things may yet go awry.

In recent years, private foundations have in large part moved away from providing grants for general operating expenses. Many foundations now focus nearly all of their attention on providing grants that are restricted to a specific purpose. More than ever before, private foundations seek to fund innovative initiatives, demonstration projects, collaborative ventures, and entrepreneurial approaches to solving community problems. So what could go wrong in this era of increased competition for grant funds by a growing pool of eligible tax-exempt nonprofits? Consider the following examples:

- ■ A community foundation announces a change in funding priorities eliminating funding for a small charity that has received annual grants from the foundation since its inception. The charity must now scramble to find a new source of support. The board of the charity questions whether staff took the funding for granted, and is dismayed that the CEO hasn't been cultivating relationships with other funders over the years.

- A foundation rejects a nonprofit's preliminary proposal for support, but offers instead to fund an alternative project. The project falls outside the core mission and programs of the nonprofit, but the nonprofit pursues the grant in order to maintain a relationship with the funder. The project consumes more of the nonprofit's resources than anticipated, and doesn't generate the hoped for additional community support for the organization.

- A small nonprofit faces an uncertain future unless it can secure new grant funds to replenish low cash reserves and provide money for operations. A foundation is willing to make a grant but requires additional information in several areas. It asks the nonprofit how it intends to address the lack of diversity on the nonprofit's board. In his eagerness to "close the deal," the nonprofit CEO describes an elaborate plan to ensure diversity. He is uncertain, however, about whether such a plan will receive support by the current board, and whether the plan is feasible.

These scenarios describe just a few of the risks associated with the solicitation and receipt of foundation funds. Other possibilities include dissatisfied funders who request that grant money be returned or refuse to fund additional projects. Most foundation grants come with very specific directions and provisions, such as:

- ❏ The grant must be expended solely in support of the objectives detailed in the funding proposal and within the approved budget;

- No portion of the grant may be used to undertake any activity for any purpose other than one specified in section 170(c)(2)(B) of the Internal Revenue Code;
- The nonprofit must track the expenditure of grant funds;
- Any press releases announcing grants must be sent to the foundation prior to dissemination;
- The funder must be acknowledged;
- The charity must maintain financial records for expenditures and receipts relating to the project;
- The charity must retain all records and other supporting documentation relating to the grant for five years after the grant's termination date;
- The nonprofit must submit midterm and final status reports containing a narrative description of goals achieved during the grant term and a financial report detailing the expenditure of grant funds;
- The foundation must be notified if the nonprofit undergoes any structural or significant operational changes;
- The grantee must permit the foundation to have reasonable access to files, records, and personnel during the term of the grant and for five years thereafter;
- The funded project must be under the complete control of the grantee and the grantee will exercise control over the process of selecting any secondary grantee or subcontractors; and
- The grantee returns on a pro rata basis any undisbursed project funds to the Foundation within a set number of months after the end of the grant.

Clearly, many of the requirements and restrictions are basic common sense, but many nonprofits simply may not have the infrastructure or storage capacity to completely comply with all of the administrative and record keeping requirements of their grants. It's important, therefore, before accepting any funds, that the organization understand what will be needed and how much it will cost to bring the nonprofit up to the standards that the foundation requires.

Typical foundation grant award letters admonish the nonprofit CEO to carefully review the terms of the award letter before signing and returning a copy to the foundation. This stage may be just as risky as the final negotiations and question and answer phase. Having worked hard over a period of time to secure a new grant, most recipients tend to gloss over or even ignore the requirements in the award letter. Such requirements are becoming more burdensome and specific. What should every nonprofit that solicits and receives foundation funding do to minimize the risk of inappropriate action?

Risk Management Checklist

- ❏ *Do not allow foundation funding to lead you astray when it comes to your mission and goals.* Changes in the world in which you operate, a change in the needs of your clients, community support and a host of other reasons are legitimate considerations in updating your mission and goals. Changing your mission or direction, however, to capture some additional funding can be a serious mistake. Changes in direction and focus should be made with the full knowledge of and in consultation with the board of directors.

- ❏ *Conduct due diligence on foundation supporters* by learning as much about the foundation's priorities and practices as possible *before* you solicit funds. It could be embarrassing to find out after the fact that the sporting goods company that gave you a large donation for your Kid's Camp program is the wholly owned subsidiary of a liquor conglomerate. Contact other grantees to learn more about the foundation's expectations of its grantees. Seek advice from other nonprofits on submitting a successful proposal, and find out how the foundation communicates with its grantees. For example, a growing number of large national foundations are limiting personal contact with grantees. Many grants are made without ever meeting with a representative of the nonprofit. This can be frustrating to a nonprofit accustomed to regular feedback and face-to-face communication.

- ❑ *Do not allow yourself to be swept up in the heat of final negotiations* on a grant and make the mistake of promising things you're unable or unwilling to deliver. It's too easy to fall into the trap of saying what you believe the funder wants to hear, rather than giving a truthful explanation of what you are capable of achieving as well as your limitations.

- ❑ *Carefully review the paperwork that accompanies a grant award letter.* Give the same level of scrutiny to the grant award document as you would to a complicated contract for services or a lease. If you are unclear about any aspect of the grant, seek clarification from the funder or an interpretation from legal counsel. Never sign an award letter whose terms are unclear. Immediately record and place on your calendar the key reporting deadlines — including those that are one or two years in the future.

Foundation grants can be an excellent way to finance innovative research or service delivery projects that require up-front capital. It is important to do your homework in the beginning, carefully scrutinize the terms and conditions you are agreeing to, and keep careful records of your finances and activities. Giving your foundation grants the attention they deserve will ensure a smooth experience with your funders, which will leave them with a positive impression of your operation and perhaps ready to provide additional funding to help you achieve your mission.

Chapter 4
Individual Donors: Roping 'Em In

From a practical standpoint, no area of fundraising has evolved more rapidly than the solicitation of donations from individuals. Less than a generation ago individuals largely contributed time and funds to their church, to the youth-serving group their child was enrolled in, at work through an organized campaign, to the person going door-to-door, or to the charity representative on the street corner at holiday time. Local businesses might display a cardboard stand with an appeal for quarters or a labeled jar on the counter. Telethons and charity advertising on TV persuaded people to give money to charities with which they had little contact and about which they had only minimal information.

According to *Giving USA 1999*, the annual report of the American Association of Fund-Raising Counsel's Trust for Philanthropy, the strong economy has been good news for charities. For the third year in a row, giving to nonprofit organizations has increased. It rose 10.7 percent in 1998 to reach $174 billion with 77.3 percent of this coming from individual donors.

The advent of direct mail and list marketing has helped to drive this dramatic growth and has changed the nature of fundraising by allowing marketing efforts to be much more targeted. The result is that it's easier to raise more money with fewer dollars. Names and addresses can be purchased and individuals who had purchased a particular product or subscribed to a magazine are sent appeals. Telephone banks and other techniques enable nonprofits to amass lists of people who are otherwise unlikely to come into direct contact with the organization's service programs.

In the last decade, the pace at which the science of individual fundraising has progressed is phenomenal. Today retirees attend seminars that combine tax planning with charitable giving. List rental by and among charities is big business, and "list brokering," matching list buyers and sellers, is an industry within an industry. Personalized direct mail appeals are commonplace, and fundraisers are increasingly drawing links between an individual's personal interests (i.e. for recreational activities, clothing, etc.) and their charitable giving preferences. Web sites with information about electronic fundraising have proliferated. Ironically, all this technology has made fundraising more complex, more expensive and riskier than ever.

Along with the technology explosion, the laws governing nonprofit solicitation and the deductibility of individual contributions have become much more complicated. The laws require donors and beneficiaries alike to keep accurate records and report extensively to the appropriate government agencies the scope of their activities.

What are some of the risks of raising money from individuals?

- Aggravating a donor by violating his or her privacy;
- Accepting a donation from an individual or organization you don't want associated with your charity, or returning/refusing a donation for the same reason;
- Projecting donations during extreme fluctuations in the economy or stock market;
- Valuing and handling bequests inappropriately; and

❑ Not conducting due diligence on donated property and valuing the benefits and costs of such donations.

Before undertaking any effort to solicit funding from individuals, a nonprofit must carefully consider the issue of donor privacy. We explore this topic and offer a suggested approach in the paragraphs below.

Donor Privacy: What is Your Obligation?

Generally, you have an obligation to respect the privacy of your donors and to tell them how you plan to use the information you collect about them. If it is your practice to collect information and to share it with other organizations (even other nonprofits), you should tell the donor how and when you will share the information. Donors should be offered the option of having their information kept confidential.

New technology is making it easier than ever to collect information about individuals and organizations. It is also making it easier for that information to be shared both wittingly and unwittingly. Remember that your information is only as secure as your computer system. For example, if your organization counsels troubled youth, the information you keep on your clients, even their names and addresses, may be very sensitive. Do not store such information on a file server or a computer that is not secure. It may be vulnerable to theft, or at the very least, prying eyes.

Providing donors with documentation and record keeping

A charitable organization must provide a written disclosure statement to donors of contributions of more than $250 or of more than $75 if it is a *quid pro quo contribution* in excess. A quid pro quo contribution is one in which something of value is received for the donation such as opera tickets, articles of clothing, even a coffee mug. More information is provided on this topic in Chapter 7.

Donations of Real Property

Only a small percentage of nonprofits are the beneficiaries of donated property, including real estate. A recent article in *The Chronicle of Philanthropy*, however, noted that nonprofits across the country are stepping up efforts to capture a portion of the estimated $20 trillion worth of real estate now in private hands. The reasons for this trend include the strength of the real estate market, making it easier for an organization to turn a real estate gift into cash. In addition, by donating property that may have appreciated in value, a donor can avoid costly capital gains taxes due upon its sale. In many cases, however, gifts of real property pose serious risks for a nonprofit recipient. These risks must be carefully evaluated before an organization considers accepting a gift of property.

The biggest area of concern is the potential legal liability if the donated property contains environmental hazards. Property that contains chemicals or hazardous waste is a problem that applies to properties other than former industrial or manufacturing facilities. A placid looking old farmhouse may harbor asbestos, contain lead paint, have stored pesticides or herbicides, or conceal leaking underground storage tanks on the premises. There may be other structures in such poor condition that they must be demolished or renovated at substantial cost. Hire a competent environmental hazard inspector to examine any property your organization has been offered and is considering accepting.

Charities should also be concerned about the potential legal liability for mishaps on the property. One real estate broker reports that as many as half of all real estate donations, which may appear lucrative on the surface, are dead-end deals or worse. Don't forget that once the title has been signed over to you, the property is yours along with all of the problems and responsibilities that may go along with it. Other risks of real estate donations may include the time and expense required to resolve partnership, lien and zoning issues, and demanding donors who may have motives other than altruism.

Risk Management Checklist

- ❑ Know the donor. Get background information on the donor. Remember that if they are audited, you may be too.

- ❑ Try to determine the donor's motivations, which often include avoiding capital gains taxes, obtaining an immediate write-off for a property that is difficult to sell, avoiding gift and estate taxes, or generating an income.

- ❑ Establish firm guidelines before soliciting real estate gifts. Develop a checklist of procedures for each transaction, such as environmental inspections, market appraisals, site visits, or title searches. Some nonprofits will not accept real estate gifts outside a specific geographical area or that are less than a certain appraised value.

- ❑ Involve your board and get expert help including the assistance of a CPA or real estate lawyer.

- ❑ Be prepared to walk away from a deal if you find that the potential costs outweigh the benefits.

Charitable Reverse Split-Dollar Transactions

If death and taxes are inevitable, as the saying goes, why not find a way to profit by them? Such is the reasoning behind some creative insurance programs that have emerged in recent years. These programs are aimed at providing a cash benefit for a charity and a steady stream of income for an individual while thwarting the tax man. On the surface, this type of arrangement sounds like a great idea — a win-win situation for everyone (except perhaps the tax man). As you may have guessed, however, things are not always what they seem. This section looks at the world of split dollar transaction insurance and reverse split dollar transaction insurance, and some of the dangers inherent in this form of fundraising.

First, what is a split-dollar plan, or a charitable reverse split-dollar (CRSD) plan, as it is properly called? The idea of a CRSD is that it allows taxpayers to accumulate assets for their family members or for their retirement by using tax-deductible charitable contributions.

There are many different ways such plans can be constructed but a typical arrangement involves an entity such as an irrevocable insurance trust which then purchases a whole life type life insurance policy on the taxpayer. The taxpayer/donor then enters into an agreement with a qualified charity where the taxpayer and the charity agree to split the costs and share the economic benefit of the policy. In other words, the transactions involve a transfer of funds by a taxpayer to a charity, with the understanding that the charity will use the transferred funds to pay premiums on a cash value life insurance policy that benefits both the charity and the taxpayer's family. Often, as part of this transaction, the charity will purchase the cash value life insurance policy. The designated beneficiaries of the insurance policy include both the charity and a trust formed by the taxpayer. Members of the taxpayer's family are beneficiaries of the trust.

In a related transaction, the charity will enter into a split-dollar agreement with the trust. The agreement will specify what portion of the insurance policy premiums is to be paid by the trust and what portion is to be paid by the charity. Although the terms of these agreements vary, the common feature is that, over the life of the agreement, the trust has access to a disproportionately high percentage of the cash-surrender value and death benefit. As part of the transaction, the taxpayer transfers funds to the charity, usually equal to the amount of premium payments that are the responsibility of the charity under the split-dollar agreement. The taxpayer will then take a charitable donation deduction for those funds transferred to the charity.

The IRS has issued a notice (99-36) to alert taxpayers and charities about certain charitable split-dollar insurance transactions that purport to give rise to charitable contribution deductions. The notice states in part:

> "Taxpayers and these organizations should be aware that these transactions will not produce the tax benefits advertised by their promoters. Furthermore, promoters of these transactions, and taxpayers and organizations participating in them, may be subject to other adverse tax consequences, including penalties."

The IRS goes on to state that "regardless of whether a taxpayer receives a benefit in return for a transfer to the charity or has the requisite donative intent, "generally no charitable deduction is allowed for a transfer to charity of less than the taxpayer's entire interest in any property."

So why should a charity care? Isn't it the responsibility of the taxpayer to make sure that any deductions are legal and above board? First of all, if your organization is promoting a scheme that is intended to circumvent the tax laws, you may be jeopardizing your organization's tax-exempt status. Even more important, consider your organization's reputation. How will it look on the morning news when your wealthy benefactor is found guilty of tax fraud and your name appears in the same headline?

Yet some of these arrangements are legitimate and may result in some benefits for your organization. Further it sometimes seems that "everyone is doing it." The key is to get sound legal and tax advice from qualified professionals to make sure you understand what you are getting involved in before you sign on the bottom line.

Taking Stock

Another popular way of soliciting charitable contributions is to encourage donors to make gifts of appreciated stock to your nonprofit organization. Such an arrangement has few risks and both the charity and the donor benefit. The donor benefits by getting the full value of the donation as a deduction (versus selling the securities first and then donating the proceeds after paying any capital gains taxes).

There are a few risks to be aware of, however. One is that you may find that your organization has unwittingly become an "owner" of a company that is antithetical to your mission. Another risk is inherent in the nature of stocks: their value changes. So a generous contribution of stock may turn out to be worthless after your organization has held it for a while.

Although the development of a sound financial and investment policy is beyond the scope of this book, your organization should have one in place and you should be prepared to bring any donations into compliance with the policy. For example, if you receive a donation of 100 shares of AT&T and your policy states that the organization will not hold equity investments, you would be required to sell the securities immediately upon receipt. If your policy permits (or if you don't have a policy), and you decide to hold the securities, be aware that stocks and bonds can fluctuate in value. Are you prepared to show unrealized investment losses on your Statement of Activity in a given year?

Because of the complexity of managing such investments, it is also wise to secure knowledgeable professional advice regarding stocks and other equity investments.

Another concern is over the kind of corporation in which you own stock. Prior to January 1, 1998, an exempt organization could not be a shareholder in an S corporation (generally a small, closely-held corporation). Although that law was amended and now allows exempt organizations to hold such stock, doing so generally doesn't benefit the exempt organization and in fact may create some negative tax consequences for the nonprofit.

IRS Publication 526 provides detailed information that is helpful to your potential donors in determining the limits on the deductibility of their contributions. See http://www.irs.gov for more information.

Baby, You Can Have My Car

It sounds like a match made in heaven. John Q. Donor has a beat up old junker that barely runs and is not worth the cost of the ad in the paper to sell it. Mr. Donor gives the car to your organization, you sell it to a junk dealer and get some money, while the generous Mr. Donor gets a hefty tax write-off for the "Blue Book" value of the vehicle. Sound too good to be legal? The U.S. Internal Revenue Service agrees with you.

At a recent conference of the American Institute of Certified Public Accountants, IRS Exempt Organizations Division Director Marcus Owens noted that automobile donation programs are "very likely" to be scrutinized by the IRS in the future. Owens is referring to donation drives held by charities where an automobile is given, and the donors of the automobiles are promised charitable deductions for the full "Blue Book" value of the car, even if the car is in extremely poor condition. According to a recent article in the *Bureau of National Affairs Daily Tax Report*, Owens said at the conference that state attorneys general are also likely to take a closer look at these types of programs.

An official used car price guide is helpful, but the condition of the car must be considered. The IRS guidelines make it clear that a taxpayer may only deduct the actual "fair-market" value of a vehicle regardless of what the "full" value may be. Of course it is the responsibility of the donor to make sure that he or she deducts only the fair market value of the vehicle that has been donated. But an organization that encourages the donor to deduct more than the vehicle is actually worth could find itself in hot water. At the very least, the organization would be guilty of questionable ethics and an organization that provides false documentation to a taxpayer may be guilty of assisting with tax fraud.

Note: The IRS requires independent appraisal certification for fair market value contributions in excess of $5,000. While it is the donor's obligation to obtain this certification, it is allowable for a charity to pay the cost of the appraisal. Form 8280 is available by visiting http://www.irs.gov.

Direct Appeals

As noted earlier, direct appeals today have become a sophisticated science. Using modern marketing techniques it is possible to send out mailings or work a phone list of potential donors who are likely to be interested in your cause. Here too, caution must be exercised. Many people do not welcome unsolicited letters or phone calls and you may end up alienating some of your best donors who have given to you in the past. In addition, there are laws and ethical guidelines that govern how such appeals should be conducted.

The Council of Better Business Bureaus has published guidelines for mail appeals, which apply to nonprofit organizations as well as for-profit entities.

Council of Better Business Bureaus Consumer Guidelines

1. Mail appeals should clearly identify the charity and describe its programs in clear and specific language. Beware of appeals that bring tears to your eyes but tell you nothing of the charity or what it's doing about the problem it describes so well.

2. Appeals should not be disguised as bills or invoices. It is illegal to mail a bill, invoice, or statement of account due that is in fact an appeal for funds, unless it bears a clear

and noticeable disclaimer stating that it is an appeal and that you are under no obligation to pay unless you accept the offer. Deceptive invoices are most often aimed at business firms rather than individuals. Contact your local BBB for detailed guidelines on how to handle appeals disguised as bills or invoices.

3. It is against the law to demand payment for unordered merchandise. If unordered items such as key rings, stamps, greeting cards, or pens are enclosed with an appeal letter, remember you are under no obligation to pay for or return the merchandise. If payment is requested, inform your local BBB. In the BBB's experience, unordered merchandise can mean high fund raising costs.

4. Appeals that include sweepstakes promotions should disclose that you do not have to contribute to be eligible for the prizes offered. To require a contribution would make the sweepstakes a lottery through the mail, and it is illegal to operate a lottery through the mail.

5. Matching check appeals are not subject to any particular legal requirements. Donors should keep in mind, however, that they do not have to return the checks if they don't contribute. The checks do not have any real value in and of themselves.[2]

The Council of Better Business Bureaus (Philanthropic Advisory Service) has also promulgated standards to promote ethical practices by philanthropic organizations. These standards are intended to be adopted by publicly soliciting organizations that are tax exempt under section 501(c)(3) of the Internal Revenue Code, and other organizations conducting charitable solicitations. The areas addressed by the standards include: public accountability, use of funds, solicitations and informational materials, fundraising practices and governance.

[2] Source: The Council of Better Business Bureaus

More information can be obtained by contacting the CBBB whose address, phone number, and web site appear in the resources section of this book. A complete copy of the CBBB's "Standards for Charitable Solicitations" appears on the organization's web site: http://www.bbb.org (click on *Philanthropic Advisory Service* on the site).

Raising Money Over the Internet

No sooner does a new technology burst on to the scene, than some enterprising person is trying to figure out how to make some money with it. No doubt the first "fire sale" occurred soon after fire was discovered.

So it should be no surprise that as the Internet has taken hold in our business and social cultures it is rapidly becoming a pervasive tool for nonprofit fundraising. The Internet is a wonderful medium for fundraising because it combines the best in visual and audio communication at a very affordable cost. In fact, the World Wide Web allows even the smallest nonprofit to have a global presence that can be as polished and professional as that of a much larger, better established organization.

There are many different ways the new technology can be used to facilitate fundraising. Most of these do not represent anything very new but are simply a way of putting a new spin on an old method of fundraising. Here are some ways organizations are using the Internet to supplement their fundraising efforts.

- ❑ Accepting contributions or membership dues on the World Wide Web and allowing payment by credit card or pledge;
- ❑ Using a web site to "distribute" promotional and marketing information about the organization;
- ❑ Using e-mail as a supplement to or instead of direct mail solicitation;

- ❑ Displaying advertising or sponsor links on a web site;
- ❑ Posting the organization's IRS Form 990 on a web site to facilitate donor retrieval;
- ❑ Conducting online sales or auctions.

Obviously, the World Wide Web can be an important fundraising tool and is one of the fastest growing methods of electronic fundraising. Using your organization's web site to create interest in your organization or solicit funds has several advantages.

- ■ It appeals to those who are already interested enough in your work to visit your web site.
- ■ It may save money since it requires no mailing, printing, or phone calls.
- ■ You can capture information about the donor for future appeals.
- ■ You can quickly reach many potential donors around the world.
- ■ Information can be quickly changed in response to circumstances.

The biggest risk in using these new strategies to augment your fundraising is that in most instances the laws regulating your actions are largely ill-defined or undefined. The U.S. Congress has thus far shied away from passing any sweeping Internet legislation. In its absence, nonprofits are faced with myriad laws from their own state and from each state in which it could be said they are doing business.

Did we mention that the Internet was global? If someone in Katmandu visits your web site and makes a donation, do you have a business presence in Nepal? You certainly do. Keeping up with all of the applicable laws in the United States alone could be a formidable challenge while, outside the U.S. could be a near impossibility.

Here are some other things that can go wrong:

❑ *The Internet does not reach out and grab your potential donors like a targeted print ad or a mailed piece.* There are hundred of millions of web sites competing for attention on the Internet. It can be difficult to generate the interest and attention your site needs to raise enough money.

❑ *Your site may experience technical difficulties.* If your web site goes down, loads too slowly or is difficult to navigate, users may get frustrated and give up.

❑ *Accepting credit card donations can create problems.* If your organization does not have a credit card merchant account with a bank or credit card company, you might be tempted to use an Internet service provider (ISP) to process credit card transactions. The ISP turns over the money to the nonprofit but keeps an agreed upon amount or percentage as a commission. This is called factoring. Charities that participate in factoring schemes may be denied future credit card services by banks or other companies. In some jurisdictions a nonprofit that factors its credit card donations may actually be breaking the law.

❑ *You may under-estimate start-up or maintenance costs and the time needed to create an effective promotion.* Creating an Internet presence is similar to adding a major new publication to your operation. A web site is a publication that may need to be updated weekly and may consume far more time than you have budgeted. It is also a task that may require more technical expertise than other projects. Do you have (or can you hire) the skills needed to meet the new challenges?

❑ *The Internet is not going to become your sole, or even your primary, system of fundraising for many years.* As you build or maintain a web site for reasons other than fundraising, however, you may want to consider developing the capacity to collect donations as part of your overall development efforts.

- One of the most common reasons for poor results from Internet fundraising is that *potential donors simply may not know about your organization or your web site.* The likelihood that someone will type your web address into a browser by chance is close to nil. Most likely, visitors to your site already know about your organization, found a link to your organization on a web site they are already familiar with, or your site appeared in the results of a search with an Internet search engine.

- Consider what other information or content you are offering on your web site. Is there a reason for individuals to visit your site other than to give you money? How often does the information change?

- Don't forget that *advertising on your web site may be considered unrelated income* just as it is in print publications. Make sure that you are accounting for such income properly.

- *Have you have allowed other organizations to use the name of your charity* on their site without appropriate licensing and other controls?

- Have you undertaken a *periodic monitoring of the Internet* to ascertain whether other charitable organizations or other entities are using your name and logo or one that is confusingly similar?

The Internet is a remarkable tool. Certainly what we have seen so far is just the tip of the iceberg, especially for tapping the potential of electronic fundraising. As with all cutting edge efforts, where the laws and practices are poorly defined and murky, it pays to be cautious and to have adequate legal counsel before venturing too far into uncharted waters.

Risk Management Checklist

Consider the following questions before you add fundraising as a function to your web site, or launch a web site with fundraising as a principal goal:

- ❑ Have you obtained legal or financial counsel on the potential tax consequences of Internet-based sales?

- ❑ Have you registered your site on all of the popular search engines to ensure that prospective donors will be able to find your site?

- ❑ Have you budgeted accurately the people hours that will be required to develop and maintain your site?

- ❑ Have you considered the risks and evaluated the benefits of a secure server for electronic transactions?

- ❑ Are you in position to reply quickly? Donors who give at Internet speed may not be satisfied with an acknowledgment sent via "snail-mail." Savvy Internet users are accustomed to instant confirmations of purchases. (Don't forget you still have to document the gift the old fashioned way for the donor to be able to deduct his gift.)

- ❑ Have you weighed the potential costs and benefits of raising money over the Internet? Is this the best use of resources?

Treating Donors With Respect

Finally, it is important to remember that donors are your organization's lifeblood and need to be treated with respect. With this principle in mind the American Association of Fund Raising Counsels, the Association for Healthcare Philanthropy, Council for Advancement and Support of Education, and the National Society of Fund Raising Executives created the Donor Bill of Rights. Keeping these rules in mind can go a long way in making sure that your dealings with your donors are consistently fair and courteous.

Donor Bill of Rights

Philanthropy is based on voluntary action for the common good. It is a tradition of giving and sharing that is primary to the quality of life. To assure that philanthropy merits the respect and trust of the general public, and that donors and prospective donors can have full confidence in the not-for-profit organizations and causes they are asked to support, we declare that all donors have these rights:

I. To be informed of the organization's mission, of the way the organization intends to use donated resources, and of its capacity to use donations effectively for their intended purposes.

II. To be informed of the identity of those serving on the organization's governing board, and to expect the board to exercise prudent judgement in its stewardship responsibilities.

III. To have access to the organization's most recent financial statements.

IV. To be assured their gifts will be used for the purposes for which they were given.

V. To receive appropriate acknowledgment and recognition.

VI. To be assured that information about their donations is handled with respect and with confidentiality to the extent provided by law.

VII. To expect that all relationships with individuals representing organizations of interest to the donor will be professional in nature.

VIII. To be informed whether those seeking donations are volunteers, employees of the organization or hired solicitors.

IX. To have the opportunity for their names to be deleted from mailing lists that an organization may intend to share.

X. To feel free to ask questions when making a donation and to receive prompt, truthful and forthright answers.[3]

[3] *Source: National Society of Fund Raising Executives*

Chapter 5
Corporate Support: Safety Net or Spider's Web?

Many nonprofit organizations have awakened to the fact that corporate support can be a good source of revenue. According to an article that appeared in the *New York Times*, corporations give more than $8.5 billion to charities annually. Although corporate support can add significantly to an organization's bottom line, it is important to look closely at a corporation's motives and business goals before soliciting or accepting money. Corporations often have a variety of reasons for contributing to a nonprofit organization. These reasons might be both benevolent and self-serving. In fact, a growing number of companies are striving to align their philanthropy and charitable giving with their business goals. Consider, for example, the manufacturer of a popular sports drink that sponsors an athletic event. Certainly, there is potential benefit in the product being associated with an event that may garner public attention. Further, there is nothing illegal or even unethical about this kind of corporate largess.

Here are some of the reasons why corporations support charities:

- A desire to support the community in which it operates;
- Shareholder pressure for charitable giving;

- To build community relations and improve public image;
- To increase consumer loyalty to their products or services; and
- To cloak their commercial product/service with the halo of credibility, respect, and trust offered by the participating charity.

Corporate givers carefully choose the projects and organizations they support. The proliferation of charities and the increased popularity of seeking corporate funds results in a competitive environment. Many corporate managers require that all charitable contributions be examined and evaluated against the business goals of the company. They consider giving to be an investment that will pay off at some point in the future through increased sales. As Nancy J. Knauer states in her book, *The Paradox of Corporate Giving*, "For them the charitable contribution must be evaluated in terms of the actual (not the potential) impact it has had on the way the company and its products and services are perceived—and, more importantly, purchased... the ultimate goal of corporate giving is profit maximization."

Many nonprofit managers are increasingly finding that corporate support is provided with strings, including the desire to be mentioned at events and in printed materials. Sponsors may request reserved seating and extra tickets, or the opportunity to offer input in staging events. Some corporations may require being the exclusive sponsor and often want substantial control over how the event is managed. Corporate sponsors generally require continuing control over syndicated rebroadcasts of the event.

Corporate funders are also realizing that corporate philanthropy has its risks. Consider AT&T's 1990 decision to discontinue its contributions to Planned Parenthood. Full page newspaper ads placed by supporters of the nonprofit decried the decision resulting in negative press for the company. Generally, corporations wish to avoid this kind of controversy.

Remember that corporations may or may not have fixed budgets for charitable giving. If the contribution is entirely philanthropic, the corporation established its budget previously and may not have any funds to allocate to your organization. In contrast, if the funding is from the marketing department, there may be more flexibility.

Before accepting corporate funds consider these factors:

- ❏ Are the company's products and values consistent with the goals of your organization?

- ❏ Will key stakeholders, including the board, other donors, or the general public have concerns or problems with the relationship?

- ❏ Will the company's presence be taken as your endorsement of the company or its product?

- ❏ Does the company expect that as a result of its donation it will have some control over a sponsored event or the organization itself? Are those expectations ones that your organization can meet?

Considering these questions before accepting corporate funding can save money, time, and embarrassment in the long run.

Just Cause: Exploring Cause-related Marketing

"Nonprofit managers can help their organizations reap the rewards of cause-related marketing alliances by thinking of themselves not as charities but as partners in the marketing effort."

— Alan R. Andreasen, *Harvard Business Review*

In the spring 1997 edition of its newsletter *"Give...But Give Wisely®,"* the Council of Better Business Bureaus notes that:

"Cause-related marketing is no longer a trend but a fund raising staple that will likely continue to flourish with possible new variations. No matter what form the promotion takes, if it is silent on how the consumer purchase specifically benefits the named charity, individuals can only wonder what the true arrangements are and will likely assume a higher portion of their dollar is going to the charity than actually is. However, pennies per purchase can still add up to significant corporate donated dollars. According to a recent poll quoted in *The Wall Street Journal*, 40% of households would give preference to an altruistic company when choosing between two similar products. This, among other things, is probably why cause-related marketing continues to gain popularity and is estimated to have raised over $2 billion for charities in 1996."

According to the CBBB, cause-related marketing is used to promote a wide range of local and national charitable programs together with specific consumer goods and/or services to create purchase-driven donations. The basic message is, "Buy the product of Corporation ABC and a contribution will be made to Charity XYZ." In general, the greater the sales volume, the more the charity gets.

With the increase of cause-related marketing, there has been a corresponding increase in the scrutiny of both government regulators and private watchdog groups. The CBBB's Philanthropic Advisory Service (PAS) has encouraged those parties entering into such arrangement to fully disclose information relevant to the consumer's purchase decision including:

- ❑ the portion of the product or service price or the fixed amount per sale/transaction to benefit the charity;
- ❑ the full name of the benefiting charity;
- ❑ the term of the campaign; and

- any maximum or guaranteed minimum the charity will receive. For example, "Corporation ABC will donate 5 cents to Charity XYZ for every purchase in the month of September up to a maximum of $500,000."

Disclosing How the Charity Benefits

As cause-related marketing becomes more common, complete and accurate public disclosures assume even greater importance. Consumers need to understand exactly how the charity will benefit from their purchases.

Increasingly, government regulators are giving closer scrutiny to such campaigns. The Federal Trade Commission instituted an enforcement action against a manufacturer of household cleaning products that allegedly failed to donate a portion of its revenues to nonprofit environmental organizations as promised. Recently, nineteen states settled actions alleging misrepresentation in advertisements for a pain relief product. One of the objections of the attorneys general was an implication that each purchase would support the charity when, in fact, purchases would not affect the manufacturer's total contribution until sales reached a certain level.

PAS also recommends that there should be a written agreement giving the corporation license to use the charity name and/or logo and giving the charity prior review and approval over any promotional material that uses its name. Of course, what is stated in the promotion should follow the actual financial arrangement agreed upon.

Even the best thought out cause-related marketing plan can have difficulties. It is important to keep in mind some of the potential negative consequences of entering into this type of arrangement.

- *Wasted resources and loss of flexibility* — You could spend lots of money and time on an endeavor that doesn't produce the results you want, leaving you with less time and fewer resources to focus on your mission.

- *Reduced donations* — Other funders may see a splashy cause-related marketing program and believe that your organization no longer needs additional financial support.

- *Tainted partners* — Even with appropriate due diligence, there is always the risk that your partner could suffer a public relations nightmare. Your name could also get dragged through the mud.

- *Antithetical marketing* — The company's marketing strategy, product line, or reputation could be inconsistent with your message and mission.

- *Overwhelming success* — The program could become so successful it becomes the dog and everything else you do is the tail. Are you a charity providing mentors for inner-city kids, or a sales force for an athletic apparel company?

- *Structural atrophy* — So much effort may be required to make this arrangement work that other departments, units, and programs start to suffer from neglect.

According to a report titled, "What's in a Nonprofit's Name," issued by sixteen states' attorneys general in April 1999, cause-related marketing efforts brought in $535 million to nonprofits in 1998. The report raises concern about the licensing of names and logos to for-profit companies and recommends that nonprofits consider the following principles when entering into business partnerships:

- Both the commercial sponsor and the nonprofit organization engaged in advertising a commercial product through the use of the nonprofit's name or logo must satisfy all applicable legal standards, including compliance with consumer laws prohibiting false advertising, unfair and/or deceptive trade practices and consumer fraud.

❑ Advertisements for commercial products must not misrepresent that the nonprofit organization has endorsed the advertised product. If such an advertisement uses a nonprofit organization's name or logo and the nonprofit has not in fact endorsed the advertised product, the advertisement must clearly and conspicuously disclose that the nonprofit has not endorsed or recommended the product.

❑ Advertisements for commercial products using a nonprofit's name or logo must:

— avoid making express or implied claims that the advertised product is superior to others in the same product category, unless the claim is true and substantiated; and

— disclose clearly and conspicuously that the corporate sponsor has paid for the use of the nonprofit's name or logo when that is the case.

❑ Product advertisements arising from a commercial-nonprofit relationship shall not mislead, deceive, or confuse the public about the effect of the consumer's purchase on charitable contributions by the commercial sponsor.

❑ Advertising partnerships between commercial and nonprofit entities should avoid exclusive product sponsorships.

Do not be afraid to walk away from a deal when you have serious doubts. No amount of money is worth compromising your organization's integrity.

This is not to say that nonprofit organizations should not enter into such agreements. With the right partner, cause-related marketing can be a major boon to your budget and give additional exposure to your organization and its goals. The key words are knowledge and communication. Understand your partners' motives and communicate your expectations. Also document the agreement in writing. With these precautions, the likelihood of misunderstandings and other difficulties will be greatly reduced.

Chapter 6
Collaborations and Partnerships: Creating a Secure Knot

Collaborations and partnerships are becoming increasingly popular among nonprofits as organizations seek creative ways to involve funders. When funders have a stake in a nonprofit's programs, they may be more inclined to support the organization on a long-term basis, or offer additional funds. The most common mistake in developing these initiatives is the failure to fully consider the risks of the project or program. A joint project with a private sector partner is not a simple corporate donation. Collaborations with government agencies and other nonprofits can be equally complex. Too many nonprofits fail to consider the ethical and risk management implications of such endeavors.

It is not only for-profit companies that are potential partners in these types of activities. Increasingly, the lines between the public sector and the nonprofit sector are blurring. Many public entities are trying to move out of areas such as social services, education, and child care. More and more, public entities are turning to contractual arrangements with nonprofit organizations to provide the services they can not provide. There may be opportunities for a nonprofit to secure long-term reliable funding for projects within the scope of its mission. Caution must be exercised here as well. Make sure that if you are providing services on behalf of the local government that your organization is protected by the government's insurance or self-insurance plan. Make sure that contracting with your organization to provide specific services is not simply a way for the government to attempt to escape legal liability.

Another opportunity for constructive partnerships lies with other nonprofit organizations. It makes a lot of sense to collaborate with complementary organizations. In times of increased competition and shrinking budgets, collaborating with another organization can be a way of conserving resources and accessing an expanded market for products and services.

It is important to remember that although your partner is another nonprofit organization, the same caveats for working with corporations and governments apply. It is just as important to proceed carefully and diligently. Here are some tips to keep in mind regardless of the type of organization you hope to partner with.

Risk Management Checklist

- ❑ *Confirm Compatibility* — Is your organization compatible with your intended partner? Will you violate any precedents or policy by partnering with the organization? For example, is it appropriate for a youth-serving agency to engage an alcohol or tobacco producer (or the subsidiary of one) as a lead sponsor of an educational program?

- ❑ *Understand Motivations* — The motivation for a nonprofit may be clear – to raise additional monies for a critical initiative. Your partner may be motivated by a number of factors, including some that may not be obvious, such as the desire to cleanse an image or to target a new consumer group, such as young adults or members of an ethnic minority group.

- ❑ *Conduct Due Diligence* — It pays to conduct a minimal level of due diligence before formalizing a partnership.

For example, is the company a subsidiary of a company that engages in activities your constituents may find objectionable? Does the company engage in unacceptable business practices (foreign labor, child labor, inadequate attention to environmental safeguards)?

- *Interpret the Message* — Carefully consider the message your constituents will receive when they learn of your partnership or collaboration. Will they be bombarded with advertising that contains your logo? Will it appear that you have endorsed a company's or another nonprofit's products or services? Have you?

- *Clarify Expectations* — The most important ingredient to a successful partnership is clarity of expectations. Make certain you know and acknowledge what your partner hopes to get out of the endeavor. If they expect an increase in sales to a specific constituency, determine what they expect you to do to accomplish that goal. Push for additional clarity beyond the simple altruistic motives your contacts may describe.

- *Put It in Writing* — Any partnership or collaboration that spans a period of time, involves a substantial sum of money (from the nonprofit's perspective), or where each partner has specific responsibilities, should be put in writing. A brief Memorandum of Understanding or Memorandum of Agreement provides an opportunity to outline expectations and responsibilities, and to assign risk to those who will be responsible if something goes wrong.

A common danger is that one or a few of the partners will end up doing most of the work, with some of the groups shirking their responsibilities or unable to meet their requirements. It is unlikely that all participating organizations are able to make their respective efforts equal.

One participant on an online discussion list recounted the following tale:

> "I consulted for a hospital endowment campaign. This hospital had for some time a very productive and harmonious service-sharing program with another hospital on the opposite side of town. Both hospitals at one time were served by a since-departed doctor who was loved and revered by both institutions. Both hospitals had started endowment raising programs in his memory and honor. I started to work with them to have them raise additional money for that fund. When the fund grew, and the income was of some real consequence, the troubles began with great arguments and great anguish regarding: Which hospital was to benefit from the endowment income? Which hospital should get the credit for the respective contributions in the first place?"

Yet another commented:

> "I know of a performing arts presenting organization (nonprofit) which houses a number of nonprofit performing arts organizations. It seemed to make sense when the presenter and two of the larger groups started a collaborative marketing effort. The good news was that all of the groups spent less to market tickets and made more ticket sales. The bad news was they began to have serious and loud disputes regarding just who owned the patrons in the seats who were now donor prospects. The dispute resulted in a dissolving of the collaborative marketing program."

With care, caution, and due diligence, collaborative efforts with other organizations can be an effective way to conserve resources and advance your organization's mission.

Drafting a Memorandum of Understanding

An effective Memorandum of Understanding (MOU) prevents misunderstandings and disputes by clarifying the expectations of the partners. The process of developing an MOU is an instructive and potentially invaluable experience in partnering. You will learn how responsive your partner will be — are your calls returned promptly? Does your partner give the partnership the attention and seriousness it requires? You may also learn how your partner reacts when you disagree on an issue. In many cases, you will learn vital information such as:

- the corporate structure of your partner (don't assume!);
- whether your partner has liability and other types of insurance;
- what specifically the partner is willing to promise (ambitious projections may dissipate as your partner commits to something realistic);
- what aspects of the project your partner is willing to be responsible for;
- how each organization will assess or evaluate the success of the project; and
- your partner's overall commitment to the project.

The refusal to put anything in writing is a red flag and may be sufficient reason not to proceed with the arrangement.

There are a number of elements that should be contained in a typical Memorandum of Understanding. Since each project and its partners are unique, the following suggestions are provided as an example. As with any contract, it is critical to obtain legal counsel before obligating your nonprofit.

1. **Overall Intent**: Many MOUs begin with a brief description of the overall intent of the parties, such as

"Whereas the mission of We CARE is to provide hot meals to homeless persons living in the District of Columbia, and the mission of We DELIVER is to deliver food to homeless persons living in the District of Columbia, the organizations hereby agree to collaborate in developing an integrated food preparation and delivery system beginning September 1, 2000."

The overall intent clause must accurately reflect what the parties are intending to do. Ulterior motives have no place in effective partnerships.

2. **The Parties**: The next clause in an MOU describes the parties to the agreement. It should generally be specific to indicate the types of organizations ("a nonprofit corporation headquartered in the District of Columbia").

3. **The Period**: Specify a time period for the partnership.

4. **Assignments/Responsibilities**: This important section of the MOU describes the duties and responsibilities of each partner. It is generally more effective to describe each organization's responsibilities separately, beginning with the items that are an organization's sole responsibility. List each group's sole responsibilities, followed by a description of shared responsibilities, if any. In many cases, this section of the agreement will be the most detailed and lengthy. Clarifying responsibilities is the number one purpose of a written agreement.

5. **Disclaimers**: Many MOUs will contain one or more disclaimers, including one indicating that employees of Organization A are not to be considered employees, borrowed or otherwise, of Organization B and vice versa. It may also be worthwhile to disclaim what the partnership is not intended to do, guarantee, or create.

6. **Financial Arrangements**: A typical partnership will have financial implications. These should be spelled out in detail

including which entity will pay for each item and when payment is due.

7. **Risk Sharing**: Another critical element of an MOU is a description of who will bear the risk of a mishap. What if something goes wrong? What if the partnership's activities result in injury, death or a financial loss? An important tenet of risk management is that an organization should never assume responsibility for something over which it does not have control. For example, a nonprofit renting a building to hold a dinner meeting should not assume responsibility for the damage caused by a leaky roof. A formal MOU may include an indemnification provision, promising that Organization A will pay for losses suffered by or caused by Organization B. Ideally, indemnification provisions should be mutual in that each party will be responsible for its own negligent acts or omissions. Remember that an organization's agreement to indemnify your nonprofit without the financial resources (including insurance) to meet this responsibility is a hollow promise. So make certain your partner is not only willing but also able to pay for losses it causes.

8. **Signatures**: A representative from each partner with authority to bind their organizations contractually should sign the MOU. Each partner should retain a copy of the signed agreement.

Chapter 7
Toeing the Line: Managing Within the Restrictions of Your Grant or Contract and the Law

Most large contributions made by corporations, foundations and governments have a range of strings attached. Few nonprofits receive "unrestricted" funding. The risks of restricted funding include:

- Failure to meet donor-imposed requirements and restrictions;
- Ineffective management of restricted funds;
- Failure to agree with the donor on benchmarks of progress toward attainment of grant purposes;
- Failure to file the correct forms with various government agencies; and
- Failure to provide donors with the proper documentation.

One concern for a nonprofit that relies on restricted funding would be that the donor might demand for the funds to be returned, or worse yet, file a lawsuit demanding reimbursement plus interest of the funds since the conditions of the funding were not met. A recent article in *The Chronicle of Philanthropy*, had the following headline: "Federal Judge Orders Brooklyn Private School to Return $3 Million Gift."

The article describes a case where a donor imposed use and time restrictions on a $2.85 million gift to a private school. The terms of the gift required that the money be used to construct a facility named the "Dr. Abraham and Pauline Kates and Dr. Edward Wasserman Building" and that it be in use as a school by December 31, 1995. When the deadline passed and the facility had not been completed, the donors sued. The school claimed that poor weather conditions had delayed construction, that it encountered difficulty raising the additional $5.5 million to complete the building, and later that three floors of one wing of a building together constituted the "school building" described in the gift document.

The U.S. District Court in Philadelphia granted the school's request for an extension on the deadline to May 15, 1997. The judge ruled that the hardship of forcing the school to repay the gift outweighed the benefits that would accrue to the donors. When the building remained unfinished in May 1997, the donors renewed their efforts to have their gifts returned.

The judge reversed his prior position, writing, "The Court is of a different mind now. Although the benefits in a tangible sense are purely monetary, the Court finds that the greater benefit... is the public policy interest in maintaining the integrity of charitable donations that are made contingent upon terms that the parties have agreed to. To refuse ever to enforce a contract because it may work hardship on the donee is quite literally to render all such contracts null and void."

Other examples of the ineffective management of restricted grants include exceeding line item restrictions in the budget, missing donor deadlines, allowing expenses to exceed revenues, or creating an infrastructure that may be insupportable once the funding cycle ends. The latter is often done with the hopes of finding replacement funds once the initial restricted grant has lapsed. A more cautious and sensible approach requires that restricted funding be regarded as temporary in nature. A detailed operational plan should be developed addressing the start-up, continuation, and ending of the funded project.

Running Afoul of the IRS

Of course it is vital for your fundraising efforts to comply with all federal, state, and local regulations. Your nonprofit, its employees and volunteers, must understand and comply with all tax laws and IRS regulations. Even "tax-exempt" organizations sometimes are required to pay taxes under certain circumstances. One of the most common types of income on which you may be required to pay taxes is unrelated business income or UBI. According to the IRS,

> "Unrelated business income is the income from a trade or business that is regularly carried on by an exempt organization and that is not substantially related to the performance by the organization of its exempt purpose or function, except that the organization uses the profits derived from this activity."

What is considered by the IRS to be UBI is not always obvious or intuitive, so seek professional help in this area. Some sources of income that the IRS frequently considers to be UBI include advertising revenue, sponsorship fees, and membership dues from "associate members" who do not enjoy the same privileges as other members. The IRS has a publication devoted to this topic, *Tax on Unrelated Business of Exempt Organizations: Publication 598,* which is available on the IRS web site, http://www.irs.gov.

Interestingly, income from programs such as affinity credit cards have recently been ruled by the courts to be royalty income which is not subject to tax (*Sierra Club, Inc. v. Commissioner*). The IRS may appeal this decision, however, so check carefully for the latest ruling before proceeding with any program.

Notifying Donors of Their Contributions

The IRS has extensive rules for providing information to donors about their contributions. It is important to comply with these regulations. The following is from the IRS web site:

Contributions to Charitable Organizations

Charitable organizations described in § 501(c)(3), other than testing for public safety organizations, are eligible to receive tax-deductible contributions in accordance with § 170.

A charitable organization must provide a written disclosure statement to donors of a quid pro quo contribution in excess of $75. A quid pro quo contribution is a payment made to a charity by a donor partly as a contribution and partly for goods or services provided to the donor by the charity. For example, if a donor gives a charity $100 and receives a concert ticket valued at $40, the donor has made a quid pro quo contribution. In this example, the charitable contribution portion of the payment is $60. Even though the part of the payment available for deduction does not exceed $75, a disclosure statement must be filed because the donor's payment (quid pro quo contribution) exceeds $75. The required written disclosure statement must:

1. Inform the donor that the amount of the contribution that is deductible for federal income tax purposes is limited to the excess of any money (and the value of any property other than money) contributed by the donor over the value of goods or services provided by the charity, and

2. Provide the donor with a good faith estimate of the value of the goods or services that the donor received.

The charity must furnish the statement in connection with either the solicitation or the receipt of the quid pro quo contribution. If the disclosure statement is furnished in connection with a particular solicitation, it is not necessary for the organization to provide another statement when the associated contribution is actually received.

No disclosure statement is required when:

1. The goods or services given to a donor meet the standards for "insubstantial value" set out in Rev. Proc. 90-12, 1990-1 C.B. 471, and Rev. Proc. 92-49, 1992-1 C.B. 987 (as updated);

2. There is no donative element involved in a particular transaction with a charity (for example, there is generally no donative element involved in a visitor's purchase from a museum gift shop); or

3. There is only an intangible religious benefit provided to the donor. The intangible religious benefit must be provided to the donor by an organization organized exclusively for religious purposes, and must be of a type that generally is not sold in a commercial transaction outside the donative context.

A penalty is imposed on a charity that does not make the required disclosure in connection with a quid pro quo contribution of more than $75. The penalty is $10 per contribution, not to exceed $5,000 per fundraising event or mailing. The charity can avoid the penalty if it can show that the failure was due to reasonable cause.

Donors taking a deduction under § 170 are required to obtain contemporaneous written substantiation for a charitable contribution of $250 or more. To be "contemporaneous" the written substantiation must generally be obtained by the donor no later than the date the donor actually files a return for the year the contribution is made. If the donee provides goods or services to the donor in exchange for the contribution (a quid pro quo contribution), this written substantiation (acknowledgment) must include a good faith estimate of the value of the goods or services. The donee is not required to record or report this information to the IRS on behalf of a donor. The donor is responsible for requesting and obtaining the written acknowledgment from the donee. Although there is no prescribed format for the written acknowledgment, it must provide sufficient information to substantiate the amount of the contribution. For more information, see *Publication 1771*.[4]

State Fundraising Laws

Another area of legal compliance that is often overlooked is the diverse collection of state laws governing organizations that solicit charitable contributions. Most states require that organizations soliciting contributions within the state register and pay a fee. Fundraising consultants/solicitors hired by a charity must also register in advance of solicitation activity, post bonds in most cases, and file copies of their contracts.

Generally, any nonprofit that conducts a charitable solicitation within the borders of a state, *by any means*, is subject to its law and is therefore required to register. The terms, "charitable" and "solicitation," are defined very broadly and may even include, for example, an Internet posting by a nonprofit organization inviting contributions from the public.

In addition, the soliciting organization need not be a "charity" in the strict sense nor have any physical presence of any kind in the state. A letter, phone call or newspaper ad requesting financial support from a state's residents is often enough to trigger the coverage of that state's solicitation law.

In spite of this rather broad definition of a charity, many states exclude a wide variety of organizations from coverage. Either through exemption from registration requirements or out-and-out exclusion from the law, each state excuses some nonprofits from registering. For example, every state grants an exemption (or exclusion) to "religious organizations," and most have exemptions for colleges and universities or for nonprofits raising only small amounts (e.g. less than $5,000).

State requirements are generally not onerous or particularly

[4] *U.S. Internal Revenue Service*

complicated, however, just keeping track of the filing requirements and forms can be a challenge. Fortunately, the Unified Registration Statement (URS) makes things a bit easier.

Most states regulate fundraising through statutes called "solicitation laws," which are primarily concerned with the solicitation of charitable contributions from the general public. Most of these regulations involve comprehensive reporting by nonprofits and the outside fundraising firms and consultants they use.

Compliance reporting under solicitation laws is divided into:

1. ***registration***, which provides an initial base of data and information about an organization's finances and governance, and

2. ***annual financial reporting***, which keeps the states apprised about the organization's operations, with the emphasis on fundraising results and practices. Typically, states require *both* registration (at least an initial registration) and annual financial reporting.

Although forty states have this type of regulation there is little consistency among states nor agreement on the uniformity of a single financial reporting document. Some states have onetime registration; others require an annual renewal; and some will require submission of various governance and financial documents. Virtually all states require an IRS Form 990 to be incorporated by reference along with certified financials above certain threshold amounts and their particular state financial report form and supplementary schedules.

The Unified Registration Statement (URS) is a joint effort of the National Association of State Charities Officials and the National Association of Attorneys General to standardize, simplify and economize compliance under the states' solicitation laws. Using the URS eliminates the need to create multiple documents for filing in many states by allowing the nonprofit to submit the same form to the states that accept it.

A copy of the URS can be downloaded from the Internet at http://www.nonprofits.org by clicking on the "Library" hyperlink. The web site also has links to the various state registration regulations as well as a summary of each state's laws, fees, and filing deadlines.

The states that currently accept the URS are:

Alabama	Missouri
Arkansas	Nebraska
California	New Hampshire
Connecticut	New Jersey
District of Columbia	New Mexico
Georgia	New York
Illinois	North Dakota
Kansas	Ohio
Kentucky	Oklahoma
Louisiana	Oregon
Maine	Pennsylvania
Maryland	Rhode Island
Massachusetts	South Carolina
Michigan	Tennessee
Minnesota	Virginia
Mississippi	Washington
	Wisconsin

The follow states require registration but do not accept the URS:

Alaska
Arizona
Florida
North Carolina
Utah
West Virginia

Summary

The Ten Commandments of Fundraising

By now you see both the importance of fundraising to your organization and the need to conduct it diligently and with care. The following "commandments" summarize the recommendations of this book and the points to keep in mind as you proceed in managing and untangling the risks of fundraising.

1. Always assess the fundraising plan, prospective donors, and partnerships relative to your organization's mission and purpose. Will the receipt of a grant or donation further enable the nonprofit to fulfill its mission and maintain its public trust? Also, does the nonprofit's request for assistance make sense in terms of the donor's mission?

2. Recognize that fundraising outcomes must grow steadily to meet basic expenses. If you are unsuccessful in growing revenues, you will be required to trim expenses constantly.

3. Pursue gifts that principally benefit the nonprofit and be wary of those where the principal benefit accrues to the donor.

4. Carefully project the cost of fundraising efforts in evaluating the worthiness of a particular activity, as well as the potential reaction your donors would have if they learn of your actual costs.

5. Acknowledge, identify, and monitor the strings attached to all donations.

6. Pursue restricted grants with caution and accept the temporary nature of all projects funded with restricted funds.

7. Proceed with caution when offered a gift with long-term restrictions (i.e. in the case of donated property, a prohibition on the future sale of the property). Circumstances change quickly in the nonprofit sector, and boards must be in position to redirect a nonprofit's resources to a more efficient or appropriate purpose.

8. Carefully monitor restricted grants to ensure that total spending does not exceed grant revenues. Avoid restricted grants that require institutional growth or projects that may not be sustainable.

9. Seek expert help from legal counsel, your CPA, or another professional, before you embark on a new fundraising strategy or activity.

10. Always conduct your fundraising with integrity and in accordance with the highest ethical standards.

Raising money for your organization is an important, complex, and time consuming task. It requires intelligence, determination, creativity, and common sense. Following the advice in this book won't necessarily turn you or your organization into a fundraising machine, but it will certainly make your efforts more successful and less risky. And while you may still regard fundraising as a necessary evil rather than the most exciting part of your job, if you are aware of the risks and pitfalls, fundraising will be a less scary and more enjoyable part of running a nonprofit organization — with no strings attached.

Chapter 8
Resources

Organizations

Council of Better Business Bureaus, Inc.
4200 Wilson Boulevard, Suite 800
Arlington, VA 22203-1804
Telephone: (703) 276-0100
Fax: (703) 525-8277
www.bbb.org

The Council of Better Business Bureaus is the umbrella organization for the Better Business Bureau (BBB) system, which was founded in 1912 and is today supported by 250,000 local business members nationwide to promote and foster the highest ethical relationship between businesses and the public through voluntary self-regulation, consumer and business education, and service excellence.

The Foundation Center
79 Fifth Avenue/16th Street
New York, NY 10003-3076
Telephone: (212) 620-4230 or (800) 424-9836
Fax: (212) 807-3677
www.fdncenter.org

The mission of The Foundation Center is to foster public understanding of the foundation field by collecting, organizing, analyzing, and disseminating information on foundations, corporate giving, and related subjects. Our audiences include grantseekers, grantmakers, researchers, policymakers, the media, and the general public.

Independent Sector
1828 L Street, NW
Washington, DC 20036
Telephone: (202) 223-8100
www.indepsec.org

Independent Sector provides information, advocacy and services for philanthropy, charities and volunteerism. The organization strives to enhance the capacity for the nonprofit sector to achieve excellence.

National Center for Nonprofit Boards
Suite 510-W
2000 L Street, NW
Washington, DC 20036-4907
Telephone: (800) 883-6262
www.ncnb.org

The National Center for Nonprofits Boards is dedicated to improving the effectiveness of nonprofit organizations by strengthening boards. The Center offers publications, education, and consulting services to nonprofit organizations.

National Council of Nonprofit Associations
1900 L Street, NW, Suite 605
Washington, DC 20036-5024
Telephone: (202) 467-6262
Fax: (202) 467-6261
www.ncna.org

The National Council of Nonprofit Associations is a national network of state-based associations that collectively represents more than 20,000 community nonprofits. The NCNA network responds to the diverse needs of community nonprofits, offering management support and technical assistance, advocacy and public education, cost-saving products and services, and professional development opportunities.

National Charities Information Bureau
19 Union Square West
New York, NY 10003
Telephone: (212) 929-6300
www.give.org

The National Charities Information Bureau (NCIB) helps donors give wisely to charitable organizations. NCIB's basic philosophy is that the public is entitled to accurate information about the organizations that seek its support. NCIB does not recommend that people contribute to one organization rather than to another, rather that well-informed givers will ask questions and make judgements that will lead to an improved level of performance by charities.

National Society of Fund Raising Executives
1101 King Street, Suite 700
Alexandria, VA 22314
Telephone: (703) 684-0410
Fax: (703)684-0540
www.nsfre.org

The National Society of Fund Raising Executives (NSFRE), an individual member association, advances philanthropy through education, training and advocacy based on research and a Code of Ethical Principles and Standards of Professional Practice. NSFRE members and affiliates enable people and organizations to better serve diverse communities and society as a whole.

Nonprofit Risk Management Center
1001 Connecticut Avenue, NW
Suite 410
Washington, DC 20036
Telephone: (202) 785-3891
Fax: (202) 296-0349
www.nonprofitrisk.org

The Nonprofit Risk Management Center is dedicated to helping community-serving nonprofits control risk. The Center offers informative workshops and seminars, publishes books, resource guides and pamphlets, and offers consulting services and technical assistance on a wide range of risk management, liability and insurance issues.

Points of Light Foundation
1737 H Street, NW
Washington, DC 20006
Telephone: (202) 223-9186
www.pointsoflight.org

Founded in May 1990, the Foundation is a nonpartisan nonprofit organization devoted to promoting volunteerism. The Foundation is based in Washington, DC, and works in communities throughout the United States through a network of over 500 Volunteer Centers. The Volunteer Community Service Catalogue offers a large collection of publications, videos, and other tools for volunteer programs.

Bibliography and Selected Resources

Andreasen, Alan R. "Profits for Nonprofits: Find a Corporate Partner." *Harvard Business Review*. November/December, 1996.

Duca, Diane J. *Nonprofit Boards: Roles, Responsibilities and Performance.* New York: John Wiley & Sons, Inc., 1996.

Greenfeld, James M. *Fund Raising Cost Effectiveness: A Self Assessment Workbook.* New York: John Wiley & Sons, Inc., 1994.

Greenfeld, James M. *Fund Raising: Evaluating and Managing the Fund Development Process.* New York: John Wiley & Sons, Inc., 1995.

Hopkins, Bruce R. *Charity, Advocacy, and the Law.* New York: John Wiley & Sons, Inc., 1994.

Hopkins, Bruce R. *The Law of Fundraising.* 2d ed. New York: John Wiley & Sons, Inc., 1994.

Scheff, Joanne and Philip Kotler. "How the Arts Can Prosper Through Strategic Collaborations." *Harvard Business Review*, January/February 1996.

Appendix A

NSFRE Code of Ethical Principles and Standards of Professional Practice

Statements of Ethical Principles

Adopted November 1991

The National Society of Fund Raising Executives exists to foster the development and growth of fund-raising professionals and the profession, to preserve and enhance philanthropy and volunteerism, and to promote high ethical standards in the fund-raising profession. To these ends, this Code declares the ethical values and standards of professional practice that NSFRE members embrace and that they strive to uphold in their responsibilities for generating philanthropic support.

Members of the National Society of Fund Raising Executives are motivated by an inner drive to improve the quality of life through the causes they serve. They seek to inspire others through their own sense of dedication and high purpose. They are committed to the improvement of their professional knowledge and skills in order that their performance will better serve others. They recognize their stewardship responsibility to ensure that needed resources are vigorously and ethically sought and that the intent of the donor is honestly fulfilled. Such individuals practice their profession with integrity, honesty, truthfulness and adherence to the absolute obligation to safeguard the public trust.
Furthermore, NSFRE members:

- serve the ideal of philanthropy, are committed to the preservation and enhancement of volunteerism, and hold stewardship of these concepts as the overriding principle of professional life;
- put charitable mission above personal gain, accepting compensation by salary or set fee only; foster cultural diversity and pluralistic values, and treat all people with dignity and respect;
- affirm, through personal giving, a commitment to philanthropy and its role in society;
- adhere to the spirit as well as the letter of all applicable laws and regulations;
- bring credit to the fund-raising profession by their public demeanor;
- recognize their individual boundaries of competence and are forthcoming about their professional qualifications and credentials;
- value the privacy, freedom of choice and interests of all those affected by their actions;
- disclose all relationships that might constitute, or appear to constitute, conflicts of interest;
- actively encourage all their colleagues to embrace and practice these ethical principles;
- adhere to the following standards of professional practice in their responsibilities for generating philanthropic support.

Standards of Professional Practice
Adopted and incorporated into the NSFRE Code of Ethical Principles
November 1992

- ❏ Members shall act according to the highest standards and visions of their institution, profession and conscience.
- ❏ Members shall avoid even the appearance of any criminal offense or professional misconduct.
- ❏ Members shall be responsible for advocating, within their own organizations, adherence to all applicable laws and regulations.
- ❏ Members shall work for a salary or fee, not percentage-based compensation or a commission.
- ❏ Members may accept performance-based compensation, such as bonuses, provided such bonuses are in accord with prevailing practices within the members' own organizations and are not based on a percentage of charitable contributions raised.
- ❏ Members shall not pay, seek or accept finder's fees, commissions or percentage compensation based on charitable contributions raised, and shall, to the best of their ability, discourage their organizations from making such payments based on charitable contributions.

- Members shall effectively disclose all conflicts of interest; such disclosure does not preclude or imply ethical impropriety.
- Members shall accurately state their professional experience, qualifications and expertise.
- Members shall adhere to the principle that all donor and prospect information created by, or on behalf of, an institution is the property of that institution and shall not be transferred or utilized except on behalf of that institution.
- Members shall, on a scheduled basis, give donors the opportunity to have their names removed from lists that are sold to, rented to, or exchanged with other organizations.
- Members shall not disclose privileged information to unauthorized parties.
- Members shall keep constituent information confidential.
- Members shall take care to ensure that all solicitation materials are accurate and correctly reflect the organization's mission and use of solicited funds.
- Members shall, to the best of their ability, ensure that contributions are used in accordance with donors' intentions.
- Members shall ensure, to the best of their ability, proper stewardship of charitable contributions, including timely reporting on the use and management of funds and explicit consent by the donor before altering the conditions of a gift.
- Members shall ensure, to the best of their ability, that donors receive informed and ethical advice about the value and tax implications of potential gifts.
- Members' actions shall reflect concern for the interests and well-being of individuals affected by those actions. Members shall not exploit any relationship with a donor, prospect, volunteer or employee to the benefit of the member or the member's organization.
- In stating fund-raising results, members shall use accurate and consistent accounting methods that conform to the appropriate guidelines adopted by the American Institute of Certified Public Accountants (AICPA)* for the type of institution involved. (* In countries outside of the United States, comparable authority should be utilized.)
- All of the above notwithstanding, members shall comply with all applicable local, state, provincial and federal civil and criminal laws.

Amended March 1993, October 1994, November 1997, November 1998

Appendix B

Standards in Philanthropy

National Charities Information Bureau
Reprinted with permission

These Standards are the result of a study in the late 1980's by a distinguished national panel. This study, which spanned two years and took hundreds of comments into account, went into full effect in 1992. NCIB believes the spirit of these Standards to be useful for all charities. However, for organizations less than three years old or with annual budgets of less than $100,000, greater flexibility in applying some of the Standards may be appropriate.

NCIB does not advise whether to give to any particular charity. Contributors are encouraged to familiarize themselves with NCIB Standards, and then decide for themselves the importance of an organization's compliance with or variation from those Standards. The information and analysis published by the NCIB is furnished to assist contributors in making informed decisions and is not intended to endorse or disparage the organization. NCIB Interpretations and Applications of some Standards are in italics.

Governance, Policy and Program Fundamentals

1. *Board Governance:* The board is responsible for policy setting, fiscal guidance, and ongoing governance, and should regularly review the organization's policies, programs and operations.

Fiscal guidance includes responsibility for investment management decisions, for internal accounting controls, and for short and long-term budgeting decisions.

The board should have:
a. an independent, volunteer membership;
    The ability of individual board members to make independent decisions on behalf of the organization is critical. Existence of relationships that could interfere with this independence compromises the board.
b. a minimum of 5 voting members;
    Many organizations need more than five members on the board. Five, however, is seen as the minimum required for adequate governance.
c. an individual attendance policy;
    Board membership should be more than honorary, and should involve active participation in board meetings.
d. specific terms of office for its officers and members;
e. in-person, face-to-face meetings, at least twice a year, evenly spaced, with a majority of voting members in attendance at each meeting;

    Many board responsibilities may be carried out through committee actions, and such additional active board involvement should be encouraged. No level of committee involvement, however, can substitute for the face-to-face interaction of the full board in reviewing the organization's policy-making and program operations. As a rule, the full board should meet to discuss and ratify the organization's decisions and actions at least twice a year. If, however, the organization has an executive committee of at least five voting members, then three meetings of the executive committee, evenly spaced, with a majority in attendance, can substitute for one of the two board meetings.

f. no fees to members for board service, but payments may be made for costs incurred as a result of board participation;

    Organizations should recruit board members most qualified, regardless of their financial status, to join in making policy decisions. Costs related to a board member's participation could include such items as travel and day care arrangements. Situations where board members derive financial benefits from board service should be avoided.

g. no more than one paid staff person member, usually the chief staff officer, who shall not chair the board or serve as treasurer;
h. policy guidelines to avoid material conflicts of interest involving board or staff;

In all instances where an organization's business or policy decisions can result in direct or indirect financial or personal benefit to a member of the board or staff, the decisions in question must be explicitly reviewed by the board with the members concerned absent.

i. no material conflicts of interest involving board or staff;
j. a policy promoting pluralism and diversity within the organization's board, staff, and constituencies.

Organizations vary widely in their ability to demonstrate pluralism and diversity. Every organization should establish a policy, consistent with its mission statement, that fosters such inclusiveness. An affirmative action program is an example of fulfilling this requirement.

2. *Purpose*: The organization's purpose, approved by the board, should be formally and specifically stated.

The formal or abridged statement of purpose should appear with some frequency in organization publications and presentations.

3. *Programs*: The organization's activities should be consistent with its statement of purpose.

4. *Information*: Promotion, fundraising, and public information should describe accurately the organization's identity, purpose, programs, and financial needs.

Not every communication from an organization need contain all this descriptive information, but each one should include all accurate information relevant to its primary message.

There should be no material omissions, exaggerations of fact, misleading photographs, or any other practice which would tend to create a false impression or misunderstanding.

5. *Financial Support and Related Activities*: The board is accountable for all authorized activities generating financial support on the organization's behalf:

a. fund-raising practices should encourage voluntary giving and should not apply unwarranted pressure;
b. descriptive and financial information for all substantial income and for all revenue-generating activities conducted by the organization should be disclosed on request;

Such activities include, but are not limited to, fees for service, related and unrelated business ventures, and for-profit subsidiaries.

c. basic descriptive and financial information for income derived from authorized commercial activities, involving the organization's name, which are conducted by for-profit organizations, should be available. All public promotion of such commercial activity should either include this information or indicate that it is available from the organization.

Basic descriptive and financial information may vary depending on the promotional activity involved. Common elements would include, for example, the campaign time frame, the total amount or the percentage to be received by the organization, whether the organization's contributor list is made available to the for-profit company, and the campaign expenses directly incurred by the organization.

6. *Use of Funds*: The organization's use of funds should reflect consideration of current and future needs and resources in planning for program continuity. The organization should:

a. spend at least 60% of annual expenses for program activities;

b. insure that fund-raising expenses, in relation to fund-raising results, are reasonable over time;

Fund-raising methods available to organizations vary widely and often have very different costs. Overall, an organization's fund-raising expense should be reasonable in relation to the contributions received, which could include indirect contributions (such as federated campaign support), bequests (generally averaged over five years), and government grants.

c. have net assets available for use in the following fiscal year not usually more than twice the current year's expenses or twice the next year's budget, whichever is higher;

Assets available for use are essentially unrestricted and temporarily restricted net assets (excluding property, plant and equipment used in operations, less related liabilities, and assets restricted to investment in property, plant and equipment) adjusted to include deferred income and exclude long-term debt.

Unless specifically told otherwise, most contributors believe that their contributions are being applied to current program needs identified by the organization. Organizations may accumulate funds in the interest of prudent management. Accumulation of such funds in excess of the Standard may be justified in special circumstances.

In all cases the needs of the constituency served should be the most important factor in determining and evaluating the appropriate level of available net assets.

d. not have a persistent deficit in net current assets.

An organization which incurs a deficit in net current assets should make every attempt to remedy the deficit as soon as possible. Net current assets are essentially unrestricted and temporarily restricted net assets, excluding property, plant and equipment used in operations, less related liabilities, and assets restricted to investment in property, plant and equipment.

Any organization sustaining a substantial and persistent deficit is at least in demonstrable financial danger, and may even be fiscally irresponsible. In its evaluations, NCIB will take into account evidence of remedial efforts.

Reporting and Fiscal Fundamentals

7. *Annual Reporting*: An annual report should be available on request, and should include:

Where an equivalent package of documentation, identified as such, is available and routinely supplied upon request, it may substitute for an annual report.

a. an explicit narrative description of the organization's major activities, presented in the same major categories and covering the same fiscal period as the audited financial statements;

b. a list of board members;

The listing of board members should include some identifying information on each member.

c. audited financial statements or, at a minimum, a comprehensive financial summary that 1) identifies all revenues in significant categories, 2) reports expenses in the same program, management/general, and fund-raising categories as in the audited financial statements, and 3) reports ending net assets. (When the annual report does not include the full audited financial statements, it should indicate that they are available on request.)

In particular, financial summaries or extracts presented separately from the audited financial statements should be clearly related to the information in these statements and consistent with them.

8. *Accountability*: An organization should supply on request complete financial statements which:

a. are prepared in conformity with generally accepted accounting principles (GAAP), accompanied by a report of an independent certified public accountant, and reviewed by the board; and

To be able to make its financial analysis, NCIB may require more detailed information regarding the interpretation, applications and validation of GAAP guidelines used in the audit. Accountants can vary widely in their interpretations of GAAP guidelines, especially regarding such practices as multi-purpose allocations. NCIB may question some interpretations and applications.

b. fully disclose economic resources and obligations, including transactions with related parties and affiliated organizations, significant events affecting finances, and significant categories of income and expense; and should also supply

c. a statement of functional allocation of expenses, in addition to such statements required by generally accepted accounting principles to be included among the financial statements;

d. consolidated or combined financial statements for a national organization operating with affiliates prepared in the foregoing manner.

NCIB may provisionally accept compilations of financial reports, if the organization has shown progress toward producing consolidated or combined statements and expects to provide such statements within a reasonable time.

9. *Budget*: The organization should prepare a detailed annual budget consistent with the major classifications in the audited financial statements, and approved by the board.

Program categories can change from year to year; the budget should still allow meaningful comparison with the previous year's financial statements, recast if necessary.